IDLE

Chess and

PASSION

the Dance of Death

ALEXANDER COCKBURN

VILLAGE VOICE / SIMON AND SCHUSTER
NEW YORK

Library of Congress Cataloging in Publication Data

Cockburn, Alexander.
    Idle passion.

    Includes bibliographical references.
        1. Chess—Psychology.   2. Chess—Biography.
I. Title
GV1448.C62   794.1'01'9   74-10751
ISBN 0-671-21817-4

Grateful acknowledgment is made to the following for permission to re-
print selected excerpts:
    Beacon Press, Inc., for excerpts from *Homo Ludens: A Study of the
Play Elements in Culture* by Jan Huizinga, © 1950 by Roy Publishers.
    The Clarendon Press, Oxford, for excerpts from *A History of Chess* by
H. J. R. Murray, © 1913 by The Clarendon Press; and for excerpts from
Soviet Chess by D. J. Richards, © 1965 by Oxford University Press.
    Dover Publications, Inc., for excerpts from *The Adventures of Chess*
by Edward Lasker, copyright © 1949, 1950, 1959 by Edward Lasker.
    Farrar, Straus & Giroux, Inc., for excerpts from *The Chess Players* by
Frances Parkinson Keyes, copyright © 1960 by Frances Parkinson
Keyes.
    Ralph Ginzburg for excerpts from his interview with Bobby Fischer,
© 1961 by *Harper's* Magazine. Reprinted from the January 1962 issue.
    International Universities Press for excerpts from "The Problem of
Paul Morphy: A Contribution to the Psychology of Chess," in *Essays in
Applied Psychoanalysis*, Vol. I, by Ernest Jones.
    Macmillan Publishing Company, Inc., for excerpts from *Man, Play
and Games*, by Roger Caillois, © 1959 by The Free Press Corporation.
    The Viking Press, Inc., for excerpts from *Dialogues With Marcel
Duchamp* by Pierre Cabanne, translated by Ron Padgett, English trans-
lation copyright 1971 by Thames & Hudson, Ltd.
    The Viking Press, Inc., and Cassell & Company Ltd. for excerpts from
The Royal Game by Stefan Zweig, copyright 1944, copyright © renewed
1972 by The Viking Press, Inc.

Acknowledgments

I have a lot of people to thank for helping this book along and for trying to keep me clear of mistakes. In the United States my friends and colleagues on the *Village Voice:* mainly Ross Wetzsteon, who first urged me into doing the book and who subsequently spent time going over the drafts; also Dan Wolt, Bartle Bull and Edwin Fancher, who read the manuscript and who suggested improvements. Also George and Jan Dillehay and Alan Weitz, who read it. In England my friends on *New Left Review*, Robin Blackburn and Gareth Stedman Jones, provided aid, notably in the historical sections. Also Dick Nations and Tom Nairn, who were in the British Museum at the same time as I. I am particularly grateful to Ian Fuller, who waded through many monographs and volumes on my behalf; even more so to Peter Fuller, who was writing his own book *The Champions*, about psychoanalysis and sport, at the same time and with whom I have spent some time talking about the subject matter of our respective books. Tony Godwin gave the book a careful reading and made suggestions. Lastly I should like to thank Emma Rothschild.

Contents

"God, I'm bored. What is it makes me feel bored? You go on living, everything is fine. Suddenly, as if you'd caught a chill, you feel bored."

— GORKI, *The Lower Depths*

*Oure days be dated
To be checkmated,
With drawttys of deth.*

— JOHN SKELTON

Introduction

In the autumn of 1972, shortly after I came from London to live in New York, I wrote a long article about chess and psychoanalysis for the *Village Voice*. No doubt because the match between Fischer and Spassky was in progress in Iceland, my account of the game in such terms aroused some general interest and, among many chess players, deep hostility. I became involved in the problems and cultural issues raised by the game.

Since readers may be curious, I had better state the extent of my own proficiency at chess. Minimal. Prodigies have a tendency to defeat their fathers at an early age, usually with traumatic results for both parties. My father defeated me in our early games. If this book were a technical treatise on chess I would be unqualified. But it is not a technical treatise. It is one of the few books on chess in which no chess diagram appears. Indeed, the reader need have little or no acquaintance with the game.

However, the fact remains that *Idle Passion* is devoted largely to chess and to chess players, artists of a game at the summit of games—the Royal Game. Chess is among the most honored of all pastimes. Excellence in chess is commonly regarded as the attribute of a powerful mind. The game allegedly reduces the intervention of chance to a minimum. It is regarded as a worthy game, even if it represents a skill and a beauty that have no meaning beyond the bounds of the game itself. One can detect a certain nervous pride in parents whose child has taken naturally to the chessboard.

Chess has another aspect of interest. Among its leading practitioners are those who have had histories of mental illness, neurotic troubles, breakdowns and the like.

Why should chess have had this effect? Or why, to turn the thing on its head, should people with such tendencies have turned to chess?

I have approached the game from a number of angles: from the case histories of particular players; from the social history of the game; from its career under the banner of national utility in the Soviet Union; from the insights of certain novelists.

I have found particularly helpful the insights provided by psychoanalysis and the concept of the dynamic unconscious. This naturally provokes indignation. There are still many people, three quarters of a century after the publication of *The Interpretation of Dreams*, who indiscriminately discount Freud. There is not much to be done about this, except hope that their numbers will decrease.

But specific deployment of Freudian theory is not my sole end in view. There are questions which, if we study one game, we must ask of all games, and of play.

How do people cope with idleness, boredom, pointlessness? What happens when they do not have to work and plot their lives around this activity?

Freedom, time, utility, chance—such concepts coagulate around the game player. Why do some players become addicted to the game of their inclination? Why does the long-distance runner torment himself with endless miles consumed each day; the racing-car driver confront death on such unfavorable odds; the gambler return to lose more; the chess player exhaust so many hours at his game? There is a remarkable amount of resistance to the analysis of motives and compulsions operating on sportsmen and game players, in so far as examination of their unconscious motives might be involved. Yet with ardent sportsmen we are dealing with addiction, and we should be inspecting its cause.

Humanism has watered the pastures of leisure and of games with much uplifting speculation. But in the world of games lie areas of darkness, of taboos, of cruel instincts and vile desires. For the time being, let us narrow the focus to the chess player face to face, as in so many medieval woodcuts, with Death.

CHAPTER ONE

The Story
of a Mere Chess Player

> "Do you know who that man is that just came in?"
> "The dandy with the monocle and the walking stick? No, who?"
> "Paul Morphy."
> "You don't mean the one who used to be the world's greatest chess player?"
> "The same."
> "But didn't I hear that he's had some kind of a terrible shock, that his mind was affected?"
> "He did have a bad breakdown; perhaps it was caused by shock. I don't know . . ."[1]

From the late sixties to the early eighties of the last century in New Orleans, a smartly dressed gentleman would promenade daily, on the stroke of noon. At the sight of a pretty face he would stop and stare. In the evening he would go to the opera. Between these regular outings he would seclude himself in his house. According to his sister he had a mania for striding up and down his veranda shouting, *"Il plantera la bannière de Castile*

15

sur les murs de Madrid au cri de Ville gagnée, et le petit roi s'en ira tout penaud."[2] He would see no one but his mother and sister, and would be angry if anyone else came to the house.

Delusions haunted him. He assumed that one of his close friends was trying to destroy his clothes; even to kill him. One day he called at the friend's office and unexpectedly attacked him. He thought people were trying to poison him; to thwart these attempts for a time he took food only from his mother and sister. At the age of forty-seven he caught a chill and died—according to some accounts, in his bath, surrounded by women's shoes. It was a sad end for one of the most extraordinary of all chess champions.

Paul Morphy was a Creole, of French and Spanish-Irish descent. He was born in New Orleans in 1837. When he was ten, his father taught him chess, and within two years he was able to defeat the best of the local players. At the age of twelve he beat, while blindfolded, his uncle, who was champion of New Orleans. At the same time he showed himself superior to two international grandmasters: Rousseau and Loewenthal.

It is alleged that he played little serious chess until he was eighteen, but during this period met no one to whom he could not give odds and still defeat. In 1856 his father died, and the following year he took part in his first chess tournament in New York. He emerged an easy winner.

Morphy thereupon left for Europe, quietly predicting to his friends that he would defeat everyone there. This he did; among his victims the strongest player in Europe, Anderssen. The feat that earned him most public

acclaim was a blindfold exhibition game in Paris against
eight of the strongest players in that city. This is how his
secretary, F. T. Edge, describes the scene when Morphy,
scarcely twenty-one, won the final game:

> Forthwith commenced such a scene as I scarcely hope
> again to witness. Morphy stepped from the arm chair
> in which he had been almost immovable for ten con-
> secutive hours, without having tasted a morsel of any-
> thing, even water, during the whole consecutive pe-
> riod; yet as fresh, apparently, as when he sat down.
> The English and Americans, of whom there were
> scores present, set up stentorian Anglo-Saxon cheers,
> and the French joined in as the whole crowd made a
> simultaneous rush at our hero. The waiters of the café
> had formed a conspiracy to carry Morphy in triumph
> on their shoulders, but the multitude was so compact
> they could not get near him, and finally they had to
> abandon the attempt. Great bearded fellows grasped
> his hands, and it was nearly half an hour before we
> could get out of the café. Père Morel fought a passage
> through the crowd by main strength, and we finally
> got into the street. There the scene was repeated; the
> multitude was greater out of doors than in the café,
> and the shouting, if possible, more deafening. We
> made for the Palais Royal, but the crowd followed us,
> and when we got to the guardhouse of the Imperial
> Guard, *sergents de ville* and soldiers came running
> out to see whether a new revolution was on the
> *tapis*. . . .

The Parisians discovered a hero and proceeded to make
the most of him. He was feted by the upper classes and
in general given more than the usual quotient of admira-
tion for a chess player.

The only player who systematically avoided playing Morphy was the reigning English champion Howard Staunton. Allegedly an illegitimate son of the Earl of Carlisle, Staunton was not only a chess master but an eminent Shakespearean scholar. He was famously bad-tempered and notoriously rude to other chess players in the chess column that he wrote.

This is Edward Lasker's account, in his charming book *The Adventures of Chess*, of what passed between Staunton and Morphy:

> Quite a number of English players expressed the opinion that Staunton would find a way of backing out of the match altogether. . . . This prediction proved to be accurate. Staunton hemmed and hawed, even insinuating that Morphy did not have the backers to provide the five-hundred-pound purse that he had stipulated. Morphy deposited the money with a London bank, and English chess amateurs, their proverbial fine sportsmanship deeply shocked by Staunton's cheap methods of evading the match, offered to back Morphy with £10,000 if necessary, to get Staunton to play. The latter finally said that his literary duties made it impossible for him to find time for the necessary training, and Morphy, disgusted, left for France.[3]

Staunton also insinuated that Morphy was a money-grubbing professional and rejected one invitation to travel to play him with the words, "The best chess players in Europe are not professionals but have other, more serious avocations." Staunton emerged from the episode without credit. He never played Morphy, and the latter, after his successful stay in Paris, returned to New York and a hero's welcome.[4]

One might have imagined that Morphy was now over the threshold of a brilliant career. He was not. He had always been extremely sensitive to charges of professionalism, and he was deeply offended by Staunton's allegations. When an official at the welcoming ceremony in New York inadvertently used the word "professional" in his paean of greeting, Morphy forced his resignation from the welcoming committee, using Staunton's own words, "Chess should not be indulged in to the detriment of other and more serious avocations."[5]

On his return to New Orleans, he tried to take up law, but he was taken the less seriously on account of his chess-playing fame. He fell in love with a beautiful young girl in New Orleans and informed a mutual friend of the fact. She scorned the idea of marrying a "mere chess player."

At the outbreak of the Civil War he hastened to Richmond to try to get a diplomatic appointment; failing in this plan he went to Cuba and then to Paris. Back in New Orleans he became obsessed with the idea that the husband of his elder sister was swindling him out of his patrimony. He spent years trying to concoct a persuasive case to prove his suspicions. It took little time in the courts to expose his charges as baseless. As we have already seen, he had paranoiac delusions of being attacked or poisoned, and a horror that his clothes, no less than his person, would be interfered with.[6]

The mention of chess was known to irritate him. Two years before he died he was asked whether he would permit the inclusion of an entry under his name in a projected biographical work on famous Louisianians. He replied indignantly that his father, Judge Alonso Morphy, of the High Court of Louisiana, had left at his death the sum of $146,162.54, while he himself followed no profession.

He did play chess occasionally, and seemed to have lost none of his skill. Edward Lasker's mother-in-law told him that as a girl she had seen Morphy on his promenades, and that he had whispered to her something about a Knight. She had felt sorry for him, since he never smiled and was evidently the victim of some great sorrow. Lasker adds that he died in his bath, taking a cold plunge after a walk in the sun.

We now come to the most renowned example of the psychoanalytic approach to chess. Although there have been many subsequent studies of chess stemming from the psychoanalytic discipline, Ernest Jones's paper "The Problem of Paul Morphy," read to the British Psychoanalytical Society in 1930,[7] remains the most famous example of a single case study. It is necessary to study it in some detail, for it was Jones's intent to discuss

> what relation, if any, his tragic neurosis bore to the supreme activities of his life, activities for which his name will always be remembered in the world of chess. . . . With our present knowledge we should find it impossible to believe that there was not some intimate connection between the neurosis, which is necessarily concerned with the kernel of the personality, and the superb efforts of sublimation which have made Morphy's name immortal.

Jones begins his explication with a few preliminary remarks about the game. Salient among them is his stress on the crucial importance of the King—the purpose of each player being the immobilization of the King belonging to his adversary. He stresses its ambivalent status as the most important yet also weakest piece on the board, the incarnation of illusory omnipotence. Etymologically the cry of "checkmate" (which, unless one player has foreseen defeat and resigned, is the announcement by the victor that he has immobilized his opponent's King) is traceable to the Persian *"shah maat"*—that is, "the King is dead."

The history of this phrase, about which there have been some amusing disputes by people reluctant to admit the evident presence of death, is as follows. The first name for chess was the Sanskrit one of *chaturanga*—literally, "four members." This was also the Indian word for "army," probably because of the four components of elephants, chariots, horse and foot. The Persians shortened the name from *chaturanga* to *chatrang*, and their Arabian successors, having neither the initial nor the final sound of this word in their language, modified it into *shatrang*. As Jones continues, "When it re-emerged into later Persian the unconscious must have been at work, for it had by then been shortened to *Schah*, an assimilation having evidently taken place with the Persian *Shah* (=King)"; "chess" thus means the Royal Game, or the game of Kings. *Shah-maat*, our "checkmate," German "Schachmatt," French "échec et mat," means literally the "King is dead." At least so the Arabian writers on chess thought, and most European authors copy them in this. Modern Orientalists, however, are of the opinion that the word *mat* is of Persian, and not of Arabian, origin and that "schah mat" means the "King is paralyzed, helpless and defeated." Again, from the point of view of the King, it makes very little difference.

Dwelling on the oft-noted status of chess as a mimicry of war, Jones remarked that "it is plain that the unconscious motive activating the players is not the mere love of pugnacity characteristic of all competitive games, but the grimmer one of father murder. It is true that the original goal of capturing the King has been given up, but from the point of view of motive there is, except in respect of crudity no appreciable change in the present goal of sterilizing him into immobility." (Of course, with the device of resignation crudity is avoided even further.) A little later Jones adds:

> The exquisite purity and exactness of the right moves, particularly in problem work, combine here with the unrelenting pressure exercised in the later stages which culminates in the merciless denouement. The sense of overwhelming mastery on the one side matches that of inescapable helplessness on the other. It is doubtless this anal-sadistic feature that makes the game so well adapted to gratify at the same time both the homosexual and the antagonistic aspects of the father-son contest. In these circumstances it will be understood that a serious match places a considerable strain on the psychical integrity and is likely to reveal any imperfection of character development. All games are apt at times to be marred by unsportsmanlike behaviour, i.e., by the sublimation undergoing a regression to its asocial origins, but with chess the strain is exceptionally great and is complicated by the circumstance that a specially high standard of correct demeanour is exacted.

Jones also deals with another feature of great importance: the rise of the Queen. He contents himself with
remarking that what was originally the *firz*, or counselor, in Persian (a piece allowed to make only one diagonal move each turn) went through the same evolu-
tion as the Holy Ghost in the Middle Ages, coming to be
known as the *regina, dame, queen* and so on. Jones concludes that "it will not surprise the psychoanalyst when
he learns the effect of the change: it is that in attacking
the father the most potent assistance is afforded by the
mother (=Queen)."[8]

After this general introduction, Jones addresses himself to Morphy's problem. He holds that the "trouble"
began with Morphy's visit to Europe. Prior to this triumphant yet fatal journey, chess had been an untroubled
sublimation of the unresolved conflicts in Morphy's personality. His enormous endurance at the chessboard (remember those ten hours without food or water at the
Café de la Régence) pointed to the depths of that sublimation, also his self-possession and confidence—"This remarkable combination of capacity and confidence could
not occur unless it was a direct representative of the
main stream of the libido and was providing the best
possible solution of any conflicts in the deepest trends of
personality."

The death of his father, Jones suggests, triggered
Morphy's eighteen-month submersion in championship
chess. He parallels it with Shakespeare's composition of
Hamlet and Freud's writing of *The Interpretation of
Dreams* after the deaths of their fathers.

So Morphy traveled to Europe to encounter the father
image, who was Staunton. (It is a slight blemish on

Jones's theory here that Anderssen was by that time the recognized European champion, but Morphy had annotated Staunton's games with some hostile comments and, we might add, echoed Staunton's own words about chess as an avocation on his return to the United States.)

Morphy failed in his objective. "The arch opponent eluded him, Morphy's aim had miscarried in dealing with this repressed hostility towards his father—and the fear of his father's towards him—by converting it into a friendly homosexual encounter." Staunton repeatedly rejected Morphy's challenges. So far from accepting the match, the object of Morphy's designs exhibited unmistakable signs of hostility. "What had appeared to be an innocent and laudable expression of his personality was now being shown to be actuated by the most childish and ignoble of wishes, the unconscious impulse to commit a sexual assault on the father and at the same time to maim him utterly: in short, to 'mate' him in both the English and Persian senses of that word."

To parallel this particular catastrophe for Morphy, Jones refers to Freud's view of the success syndrome, where fantasy disastrously blends into reality, and the castration of the father in dream becomes unbearable reality. At any rate the mental and moral stability that underlay Morphy's sublimation was wrecked, and the tensions that lay beneath were exposed. Chess sublimation ceased to act as a defense function, even though the actual capacity of chess playing used in the sublimation remained.

Worse was to follow: so far as love was concerned, his suit was rejected because he was a "mere chess player"; and through a combination of circumstances he never got anywhere with his chosen career as a lawyer. As Jones says:

> In the two things that comprise manhood, a serious career among men and the love of women, his chess past dogged and thwarted him. He was never able to escape from the "sins" of youth and to take his place among the world of men. Little wonder that his abandonment of chess became increasingly complete till he loathed the very name of it. The only recourse left to him in attempting to deal with his burden of guilt was to project it. In the delusions of being poisoned and robbed we recognize the oral and anal-sadistic fantasies projected on to his sister's husband. His homosexual friendliness to men had broken down and the antagonism underlying it lay exposed. This merged in the direction of his brother-in-law, evidently a substitute for his father, while the last anecdote of his life (his refusal to appear in the biography of eminent Louisianians) shows how he clung to the exaltation of his father, to whom was reserved the patriarchal privilege of "making money."

In addition, the mimicry of battle in chess became the reality of the Civil War, which Morphy attempted to flee. His career wrecked by chess, as also his prospects of marriage, there remained to him only seclusion and paranoia.

Such, in essence, was Jones's interpretation of Morphy's life, and his version of the "meaning" of chess. He held that the game itself concerned father murder and that the impulses that drove an addicted player forward were mixed, though the essential motor was libidinal. "I conceive that the parricidal impulses were 'bound' by an erotic cathexis, actually a homosexual one, and that this in its turn was sublimated." Chess, in this version, performed the healthy function of transforming sexual aggressiveness and thus protecting the ego. What happened in Morphy's case was that after his trip to Europe chess ceased to exercise its sublimating power.

It needs to be said first about Jones's paper that it does advance a *theory* about Morphy's descent into psychosis. At the start of the paper Jones had stressed that there must be a connection between Morphy's skill at chess, and his subsequent mental afflictions. With pleasing brevity Jones set about showing what this connection was. Such an attempt, whatever one might think of its success, can be contrasted with much lay comment about Morphy's case. For example, Al Horowitz, in his *The World Chess Championship*, has this to say: "Whether in fact chess drove him mad, or his hatred of the game was merely a concomitant of his madness, is of course impossible to determine."[9] It is a little surprising that Horowitz, the chess editor of *The New York Times*, and three times U.S. Open Chess Champion, should find no space even to mention Jones's celebrated addition to chess literature. (One could note, apropos the hostility of chess players to psychoanalytic comment on the game, that patients often fear that analysis will take their sublimations away by revealing their defensive function. Jones concludes his essay with this point.)

Naturally, in his zeal to emphasize the central point of his observations—namely, chess as a ritual of father murder—Jones simplified certain points and perhaps laid insufficient emphasis on others. For example, it is clearly of profound significance that Morphy was a prodigy. Prodigious skill in any field is bound to be disorienting for the prodigy, since many of the sanctions and regimental functions of the parent and the teacher cease to apply. The father is flung into a state of neurotic apprehension at the sight of such invincible talent. If chess is a sublimation of parricidal impulses, the actual game with a father must be of great emotional intensity, and victory must be an intensification of unconscious guilt.

Again, in an effort to gain clarity of impact, Jones gave short shrift to the social causes of Morphy's neurosis, a failing that has generally characterized the psychoanalytic literature on chess. It is amusing to contrast Jones's brief mention of Morphy's rejection by the girl he hoped to marry—on the grounds that he was a mere chess player—with the account given in Frances Parkinson Keyes's novel *The Chess Players*, the central character of which is Paul Morphy.

Miss Keyes, to judge by the length and detail of her bibliography, had immersed herself in the literature, social history and contemporary documents of New Orleans during Morphy's life. She claims that all the events in the book are based on fact, with the exception of her portrait of Morphy's beloved, Charmian Sheppard. But she claims to know who this girl was, and to judge by her instincts in other portions of the book, her judgments of social mores and social tensions in New Orleans are probably sure; her account of the rejection scene is delightful, and in view of psychoanalytic speculation about Morphy's homosexual tendencies, quite perceptive:

"I'm a Yankee," she said, "a storekeeper's daughter. Don't you suppose I know that's what your people have been calling me all these years? They think I'm not good enough for you. Well, it's the other way around. You're not good enough for me. What have you ever done but play chess? Have you ever earned a cent yourself? Do you ever expect to? I want a man who amounts to something, a man who's a success, like my father. Oh, I know you've won prizes, that stuffy, snobbish people, like the ones you're staying with and who gave you that dinner last night, fawn over you and flatter you; but when you come right down to it, what does that amount to? Nothing, absolutely nothing!"

"Charmian, you can't mean what you're saying! I realize I'm not worthy of you, no man is, but I'll try to be! And you have accepted me as— ˀˀ a sweetheart for years! You have given me to understand—"

"I've just said, I *like* you as a sweetheart! You can kiss me if you want to and I'll kiss back, but I never meant you to understand that kissing and—and things like that necessarily meant marriage. Perhaps, you *could* have married me, if you'd really tried, if you'd 'forgotten yourself,' as you once said long ago you were afraid you might, and swept me off my feet. But you didn't, either then or later. You went on playing chess. Afraid! You needn't have been afraid! All you had to do in Paris was to go a little further—so far I couldn't have stopped you if I'd tried and I wouldn't have tried very hard. You might have known that. If no one found out, what difference would it have made? And if anybody had found out, my father would have been the very first to say there'd have to be a wedding right away. He'd have stood by me, he'd have given us all the money we

needed, so that we could be comfortable and independent of your family. But it would have taken
something like that to make him. And nothing like
that has happened. I know now that nothing will.
. . . And I may as well tell you, now as any other
time, that I'll never marry a mere chess player!"

An excellent scene. Seldom has rejection on the basis
of class and inadequate sexual energy been more pithily
expressed. It's fiction, but there is exactitude in Miss
Keyes's treatment of chess as an emblem of idleness, and
sublimated energy. Throughout the novel, her treatment
of Morphy's delicacy of manners is sure. Charmian
shouts, "You needn't have been afraid!" But why was
he? Charmian's answer is, Chess. In a remarkable,
though perhaps unintentional, portrait of the ferocity
of Morphy's drives, Miss Keyes eventually has Morphy
make a final tryst with Charmian, in which he hopes to
extricate her from an unhappy marriage with a sadistic
French marquis. Morphy creeps into her house late at
night, lured by a false note. He parts "the rose-colored
curtains" around "the great golden bed" which is "her
secret realm of love." "She was lying naked on blood-
stained sheets. . . . Nothing remained of her beautiful
face but a pulpy mass of battered flesh. She had been
beaten to death."

Given the sexual imagery of rose-colored curtains,
golden bed, and secret realms of love, it seems to me
reasonable to suppose that the real meaning of the
words is that Morphy—in the *alter ego*, or Hyde part
of his character—ravished Charmian and then sadis-
tically murdered her. Miss Keyes had read extensively

in the literature and times of Morphy and presumably cogitated long on his character. She had—to judge from some of her notes—read the essay by Ernest Jones. Therefore, although her portrait of Morphy is extremely favorable to him, it is interesting that this account of the death of Morphy's sweetheart should have been, in her narrative, the reason for Morphy's suffering a nervous breakdown. In short, Morphy's misery had many mansions. Seldom has the avocation of chess taken so thorough a revenge.

CHAPTER TWO

Paths of Exile:
Nabokov's Grand Master

There is a poignant moment in Renoir's film *La Marseillaise* when the director suddenly transfers us from the revolutionary tumult of Paris to an exile's drawing room across the Rhine. In a melancholy little salon some *émigrés* have gathered to plot and to remember the good old days now gone. One of the girls sings a short song, and when she is done there is a pause. No one can speak, so bitter is the present, so remote the former times. The exiles keep enacting rituals, endless repetitions of word and custom, both to retain the past and to blunt its anguish.

This repetition compulsion, which Freud considered to be the soul of order, is a familiar feature of those who are desperately trying to maintain an order they fear or know may have broken down. It is particularly familiar among exiles: repetition becomes an umbilical cord connecting them with home, with childhood. What is heightened in the case of exiles is generally true of all people, in the increasing exile from their own childhoods; and the process starts in childhood itself.

Most parents will have noticed the curious phenomenon of a child apparently repeating an unpleasant experience—such as a visit to the dentist. Is the child's manipulation of the imaginary drill merely a mimicry, a fairly meaningless adaptation of excess energy to a recent experience? Robert Waelder, in his article "The Psychoanalytic Meaning of Play" remarks that "a painful experience is repeated in play, not after it has been overcome and mastered, but before, while it is still unmastered."[1] In a sense the child is enjoying a leave of absence from reality—the case in many games and forms of play—but the leave of absence has great significance in relation to the child's real life.

Now, the game of chess has much to do with repetition —repetition with variation certainly. Yet the player will repeat, and repeat again certain moves; he will replay throughout his life certain gambits and strategies; in his own form of exile from reality he will repeat certain rituals that may have the same fundamental significance as the child's toying with the imaginary drill. The chess pieces represent a mime of the Oedipal situation, and the player is forced to confront this mime every time he looks at the board. The player may be receding in time from a traumatic event, yet in the game he plays each day, that event enjoys a symbolic repetition or metaphoric existence in the battle of the pieces. The player is exiled from his childhood as the years go by; he is exiled from ordinary reality during his chess séance; yet that exile allows him to play out the dramas of his early life, otherwise repressed.

Nowhere is there a more striking illustration of these

ramifications of the game than in a novel by an avowed enemy of Freudian ideas—Vladimir Nabokov. One of Nabokov's greatest novels is *The Defense*.[2] It is the story of the life and death of a chess master, Luzhin. Let us examine now, in some detail, the game Nabokov, an exile, plays with his exiled grand-master.

Luzhin is born into a middle-class Russian family toward the end of the last century. His father writes boys stories, and little Luzhin spends many of his early years as the uncomprehending and unsuitable object of his father's hopes. "Luzhin senior, Luzhin who wrote books, often thought of how his son would turn out. Through his books . . . there constantly flitted the image of a fair-haired lad, 'headstrong,' 'brooding,' who later turned into a violinist or a painter, without losing his moral beauty in the process."

The ironies of expectation lie at the root of many of Nabokov's paradoxes throughout the novel. Fate plays the cruelest of jokes on Luzhin senior. There comes a day for little Luzhin "when the whole world suddenly went dark, as if someone had thrown a switch, and in the darkness only one thing remained brilliantly lit." Chess. It comes, crucially, on a day when little Luzhin's aunt has been flirting with his father. His mother has fled from the room in tears, and in the study the aunt first shows Luzhin how to play chess—"and this is how one piece eats another, as if pushing it out and taking its place."

Luzhin has been born with a talent—the aptitude to play chess. It takes the sight of his mother being betrayed, the apprehension that his attractive aunt will push her out and live with his father, to trigger that talent, to throw the switch. His aunt and father are combining; the therapy is chess, but the therapy and sublimation retain the imprint of the trauma even as they mollify it. An added element is Luzhin's own combination with the attractive aunt; she teaches him the game. His jealousy against his father is on a double level: the father not only has his mother; he has captured the aunt as well.

Luzhin is a prodigy. Whereas life has been, so far, a journey of inert anguish, the game soon offers him a significant victory. He plays his father for the first time. The father is astounded by his son's passion, it "seemed so unexpected—and at the same time so fateful and inescapable." And as the father plays he cannot stop thinking of the day he has spent with his wife's sister. The game goes on for only a few minutes before his son explains that there is no way the father can avoid defeat. Luzhin senior quickly loses the game, then two more, and he realizes that such will always be the case.

His pleasure in this revelation of his son's talent is equivocal, his aggression at his son's superiority never entirely dissipated. Years later, exiled in Berlin and his son in the hands of a foster father impresario who has touted him about Europe, the father still has not come to terms with his son's specific and distressing talent. He contemplates writing a novel about his son's career but cannot avoid transferring him in his imagination into a romantic, pallid musical genius rather than the taciturn games player who occasionally visits him. One thing he is determined on, as he broods on the fictional son he is creating: " 'He will die young,' he said aloud, pacing restlessly about the room."

Luzhin, the prodigy incompetent in ordinary social life, penetrates further and further into the satisfactory universe of his talent—"Real life, chess life, was orderly, clear-cut and rich in adventure, and Luzhin noted with pride how easy it was for him to reign in this life." But the further Luzhin becomes exiled from the traumatic day of his initiation, the more prosaic and uninventive his actual match play becomes. It is as though he cannot press too far into "chess life" without losing something. As we all need to dream, so Luzhin needs his dream of life, to reinforce the strength and purity of his play. He has to poise himself just on the pivot between life and play. The tensions involved in this kind of balancing act are intolerable.

The crisis approaches as Luzhin enters the crucial tournament in Berlin. He starts to fall in love. For the first time he has some "life" to visit at the end of the day's play, instead of a hotel room and more chess study. Day after day he plays; evening after evening he visits the home of his fiancée, a home which her exiled parents have rendered into a kitsch memento of old Russia.

This evocation of the scenes of his childhood obliterates any distinction between the real world and his own chess world. Worse, when he talks to his fiancée's mother about marital prospects he keeps seeing a shadowy chess game in progress on the checkered floor of the drawing room; he even tries to "remove shadow's King from the threat of light's pawn." Everything outside chess turns into fantasy, a dream set entirely in the Russia of his childhood. "Luzhin noticed this return to Russia with interest, with pleasure. It diverted him especially as the witty repetition of a particular combination that occurs,

for example, when a strictly problem idea, long since discovered in theory, is repeated in striking guise on the
board in live play."

The crucial tournament for which Luzhin is in Berlin
progresses, and he plays better than ever before. It is as
though he can really utilize his talent only when his
chess life is buttressed by the return of an old combination in his life—the Russia of his childhood, the threat of
real life.

In the last round, when he is playing for first place
with Turati, he finally becomes entirely submerged in
chess. The exterior world ceases to have any reality. He
burns his hand with a match. "The pain immediately
passed, but in the fiery gap he had seen something un-
bearably awesome, the full horror of the abysmal depths
of chess. . . . There was horror in this, but in this was
also the sole harmony, for what else exists in the world
besides chess? Fog, the unknown, nonbeing . . ."

Horror in life, horror in chess: the former is a tortuous
and painful puzzle, the latter a horrible journey toward
the absolute. But in both spheres there is one absolute:
time. As Nabokov remarks, when Turati is playing, toward the adjournment of their great game, "Time is
merciless in the universe of chess."

Luzhin, still lost in his chess world, blunders out of the
café after the game has been adjourned. In the outer sub-
urbs of Berlin, amid drizzle and darkness, he thinks he
can make out the mill house and the stream where he
played as a child. Infancy and chess alone have reality.
Everything else is a world of phantoms. He suffers a
complete breakdown. His legs feel weighted, like the

base of a chess piece. Weight on his skull becomes intolerable, and he collapses.

He awakes in hospital, on the first stage, as it were, of a replay of his entire life, but this time a replay in which it is hoped that chess will play no part. " 'Horror, suffering, despair,' said the doctor quietly, 'these are what this exhausting game give rise to.' 'I shall stop loving you,' said his fiancée, 'If you start thinking about chess.' "

She is trying to continue his father's fantasy—the re-creation of a Luzhin removed from the single zone in which his life has found coherence. They suffer from the same illusion, that his talent is a general one and that it is only by unhappy accident that it has been exercised in the practice of chess.

Nabokov has Luzhin move to and fro on a seesaw; the search is for some sort of equilibrium. With the arrival of Luzhin's madness he gives him the fictional equivalent of shock treatment: he regains the life of his childhood, at the price of the loss of his chess life. But now this repressed zone begins to return to him; and as he plods his path through marriage and plans for a healthful trip abroad, he begins to remember more and more of the sequence that led him to his first confrontation and immersion in chess. Nabokov introduces this phase with a little echo of an earlier remark: "Just as some combinations, known from chess problems, can be indistinctly repeated on the board in actual play, so now the consecutive repetition of a familiar pattern was becoming noticeable in his present life."

Luzhin develops a dreadful sense of the uncanny, of *déjà vu*. He begins to imagine that he is repeating the entire game of his life, and that the outcome holds something horrible for him. The sense of repetition is horrifying. He is tempted to "stop the clock of life," to seek an adjournment.

He begins to have the belief, familiar in many cases of paranoia, that the only way to outwit his opponent is to make an "absurd move," a surprise defense that would nonplus his enemy. But every move he makes seems to return him to the game, and he realizes that the object of this game is to return him to the world of chess, from which he has temporarily escaped. "By an implacable series of moves it was leading once more to that passion that would destroy the dream of life. Devastation, horror, madness."

What can he do? He decides, as he bows a smiling farewell to his wife, that he has, literally, to drop out of the game.

Through the lavatory window he clambers and for a moment hangs there. He sees the void below him dividing into "dark and pale squares" and as he falls he sees "exactly what kind of eternity was obligingly and inexorably spread out before him."

"The door was burst in. 'Aleksandr Ivanovich, Aleksandr Ivanovich,' roared several voices.

"But there was no Aleksandr Ivanovich."

In his plunge, Luzhin recovers, for the first time in the novel, his full name and at last fully enters the exclusive world of chess: nonbeing.

Thus, Nabokov studies the player and the game. The theme of exile winds ironically through the tale, and so does the theme of repression, of liberation from trauma and repression in chess, but also the breakdown of this sublimation—"fog, the unknown, nonbeing" versus the "abysmal horrors of chess." Sublimation becomes nemesis, as the chess moves that Luzhin makes throughout the book lead him toward the bathroom window from which he plunges. The absurd nonlife can only end with death.

Nabokov conducts a kind of parody on the idea of "the game"—specifically the game of chess. Chess, as I have said, is often taken as a symbol of mental prowess, a label of distinction. But outside his own field of talent Luzhin is entirely helpless, a kind of vegetable. The game that seems to rescue him from the miseries of early childhood has a kind of "auto-destruct" built into it. The unnatural, pure world it opens up to Luzhin embodies perfection, the only receptacle for what Nabokov calls "the sterility of his recondite genius"; but there is a price to pay.

One theme we will examine in the next chapter: the actual nature of the sublimation that Luzhin finds in chess. Nabokov, despite his sneers about the "Viennese delegation"—i.e., psychoanalysis—seems to wish to make it clear that Luzhin's "recondite genius" is reinforced by the circumstances of his childhood; that the day he discovered chess was also the day he witnessed, however uncomprehendingly, evidence of a liaison between his father and his aunt. His chess life is to be a flight from that initiation. Yet his sublimation can never dispel the original trauma. Thus Luzhin's dreadful panic when he suddenly imagines that his life has become a repeated game; that he must always play with the same pieces; that no combination, however dazzling, can rescue him, except "sui-mate."

It remains to stress one thing: that the actual game of chess is more than a mechanism, that it is a participant among all the other characters. The game takes its revenge on the people who play it. The stories are about displacement, about exile, about the return of the repressed; "the playful repetition" of despair and pain.

Is this novel an idiosyncratic fiction, or is the game always the repository of violence, neurosis, grief, familial crisis, death? More seriously, if chess is taken as the "game of games," the perfection of one form of play, what does its career and the fate of its leading practitioners tell us about play and about games; about their place in society and the use to which society has put them?

The career of chess has extended over more than a thousand years. It has commanded extraordinary addiction among enthusiasts, and they have made extraordinary claims for its virtues. By and large, its devotees refuse much speculation about its "meaning" and why they should play it with such ardor. They do say that "it is beautiful," that "its riches are inexhaustible," even that it is useful. This does not seem to be quite good enough. Every activity in which people frequently indulge has its "meaning," whether for the poker player, the roulette enthusiast, the tennis champion. The more remote such avocations are from social norms, the more open to question becomes the reason for that person's enthusiasm or addiction. Questions posed by Nabokov in fiction can become questions posed—sometimes impertinently—in life.

CHAPTER THREE

Splendors and Miseries of the Great Chess Champions

Morphy was real, Luzhin imaginary. Their fates can excite sympathy and promote speculation. But we need more evidence, more details than those provided in Ernest Jones's single paper. It is all the more interesting, therefore, that the first substantial development of Jones's ideas should have come from someone who was a grand master as well as a psychoanalyst.

Reuben Fine is one of the best chess players the United States has produced. In the late 1930s he was within reach of the World Championship. With the onset of the Second World War he gave up championship chess. During the war he had his aptitude for chess put to military use. He was employed by the United States Navy to calculate, on the basis of positional probability, where enemy submarines might surface.

After the war he became—and still is—a practicing psychoanalyst. His essay "Psychological Observations on Chess and Chess Players" is deeply instructive. Jones re-

garded it as an "important extension" of his own essay
and considered it a classic.[1]

Fine accepts Jones's ideas as a starting point, but he
expands and develops them. He agrees that

> chess is a contest between two men in which there is
> considerable ego involvement. In some ways it cer-
> tainly touches upon the conflicts surrounding aggres-
> sion, homosexuality, masturbation and narcissism,
> which become particularly prominent in the anal
> phallic stages of development. . . . Genetically, chess
> is more often than not taught to the boy by his
> father, or by a father substitute, and thus becomes a
> means of working out the father-son rivalry.

Fine adds, incidentally, that very few chess experts have
sons who are also strong players; unconsciously the father does not permit the identification to take place.

Like Jones, he lays emphasis on the overriding importance of the King in the symbolism of the game—a piece
indispensable, yet weak.

> It stands for the boy's penis in the phallic stage, and
> hence rearouses the castration anxiety characteristic
> of that period. It describes certain essential character-
> istics of a self image and hence would appeal to those
> men who have a picture of themselves as indispens-
> able, all-important and irreplaceable. In this way it
> affords an additional opportunity for the player to
> work out conflicts surrounding narcissism. It is the
> father pulled down to the boy's size. Unconsciously it
> gives the boy a chance to say to the father: "To the
> outside world you are big and strong, but when we
> get right down to it, you're just as weak as I am."

Pawns, simulacra of children (*spawns*, as a matter of fact), have a destructive relationship to the father (King) whom they cannot replace. The Queen (mother) is instrumental in attacks on the King.

Fine concludes that the chessboard is a mime of the family structure, and that the obsessional fascination with which players become immersed in the game is explained by the proximity of the mime to the family drama, as the player constructs relationships and on the board accomplishes revenges which are denied to him in real life.

Where Fine develops in a slightly different direction from Jones is in the arena of ego as opposed to id psychology. From this point of view he discusses the vexed topic of what the attributes of a good player are. According to Fine, four aspects of intelligence predominate in chess: memory, visualization, organization and imagination. Above all, thought replaces action in the deployment of these talents. Intellectualization is all. There is even a taboo on touching the opponent's pieces, unless for capture. In all serious chess (which is the only kind of chess there is) a player may touch his own pieces only for the purposes of making a move. The tense etiquette surrounding a player's touching of a piece can be attributed to two precautionary measures by the ego, Fine suggests. It is "explaining" or dismissing two suspicions: that the player is masturbating, by touching his piece; or making a homosexual overture, by proposing physical contact between the players, or mutual masturbation.

The Dutch psychologist de Groot likened the thought process of the player to that of the scientific researcher, constantly exploring—in the case of chess with only one permitted experiment each turn—various hypotheses, forced eventually to make one or another decision. Fine does not entirely accept the purposive nature of a chess player's thoughts. He says that much of the time, when the next move lies with his opponent, the chess player is daydreaming, and his thoughts often are not concerned with chess at all. But even in the middle of an irrelevant reverie the player is under some tension, because he knows that this dreaming will have to be abandoned when it is his turn to make a move, and that he will have to desert dreams for "feverish uncertainty and intense searching." The chess player, therefore, differs from the daydreamer or schizoid in the sense that the game in which he is engaged does not allow him unconstrained fantasy.

As Nabokov said, time is merciless in the universe of chess. Fine's remarks are also absorbing as an insight, based on experience, into what sort of "high"—to use a modern idiom—the chess player really enjoys. The conventional idea, after all, of the chess player is of a thinker lost in calculation—no time for the idle dream and fleeting thought. But then Fine says that the idle dream and fleeting thought are the substance of the player's brooding. His "leave of absence" is a leave indeed, qualified by this urgent necessity to confront from time to time the reality of the game, and finally, at its conclusion, to return to the reality of life.

The player uses abilities that require a high degree of ego development. Aggression is deeply repressed. The player must conceal from himself his *basic* ambitions in the quest for checkmate: castration, exposure of the concealed weakness, destruction of the father. And as players become more expert, checkmate is diluted into mere resignation.

It is important to remember that not only does the chess player's ego sublimate and intellectualize aggression, it provides some gratification for it in the game itself. Fine says that one prison psychologist noted that prisoners who learned chess in prison were less likely to be recidivists.[2]

The question of homosexuality must arise in a situation where, as Fine puts it, "two men are voluntarily together for hours at a time with no women present." He adds that there is almost no evidence of overt homosexuality among chess players, since the rituals and symbols of the game gratify such desires on the level of fantasy. "Checkmate may be seen as rendering the father impotent, again part of the homosexual complex." But the fact that such desires are gratified on a fantasy level does not annul the anxiety that is ever present. By his own wit the player accomplishes victory or suffers defeat. Victory implies victory over the father; loss implies submission or defeat at his hands. Thus, the player fears retribution for his active role in the Oedipal conflict.

Two more important traits are to be emphasized: narcissism and hero worship. A victory in the game implies victory over a King, and the player may suffer from megalomaniac delusions. Furthermore, the figure of the King may encourage traits of hero worship. "The capacity to achieve true object relations, particularly to empathize with women, is underdeveloped." Thus the player will enjoy the company of men, since chess represses and satisfies impulses of aggression and homosexuality; but he will discover no such liberty in his relations with women, and this may reinforce feelings of misogyny.

Finally, on the topic of voyeurism-exhibitionism—it is unconscious and gratified by a two-man situation. A chess player is apt to feel uneasy in crowds, and because of the added narcissistic factor, indifferent to organized groups. The ego weakness lies primarily in this narcissistic fixation, which makes it hard for the man to emerge from the homosexual to the heterosexual stage of development.

Fine follows Jones in having much to say, but with greater emphasis, about Morphy's constant stress on chess as a recreation, not a profession. He subsequently refused to take up any other profession. Since he was champion of New Orleans at the age of twelve, and champion of the world at twenty-one, the major portion of his life between those two dates must have been spent playing chess. So far as is known, he had few, if any, sexual experiences. Everything was abandoned in favor of chess—and this warded off psychosis. But, as world champion, Morphy could no longer take chess lightly. It could not be recreation; it lost its defensive value. A further regression took place, and the psychosis, previously concealed, broke out in full force.

Morphy, as Fine points out, preserved far more casual games than usual; and he suggests that they must have been kept with exhibitionist intent. Fame, in his mind, threatened to expose this exhibitionism. Only a regression could rescue him from the danger. Furthermore, Morphy, though by no means the all-time genius he has subsequently been termed, did have the ability to see combinations clearly, and he had an intuitive realization of the importance of position play. In his psychotic stage, Morphy became signally overorganized in every aspect of his life—a walk at noon, an afternoon with mother, opera each night.

Morphy was famous for his gentlemanly behavior at chess—that is, his complete repression of aggression. A further repression took place in his psychosis, punctuated by the homosexual assault on his friend, who allegedly took his clothes—that is, "unmasked" him. His voyeurism was gratified by the opera and the business of the women's shoes.

Now it might surprise people—though not, I think, chess players—to be told so consistently, in this type of examination of chess, that it is a sublimation of aggression. Sublimation, after all, is a palimpsest of the repressed or sublimated material: is it then so evident that chess contains deep elements of aggression? There is ferocity as mimed in the sedate operations of play. Players themselves will tell you that they feel "destroyed" or "smashed" when they have been defeated, or feel an equivalent sense of victory if they have triumphed. But even this admission falls short of acceptance that there are profound reasons for such emotions; it is, furthermore, unlikely that the panorama that Jones and Fine present is likely to be acceptable to those who cherish the game of chess. (There is an irony here, in that Jones and Fine were both passionately fond of the game.)

Few players will believe in the idea that they are sublimating parricidal or homosexual impulses, or that they are indulging in a mime play of the family drama. There is the added reservation, expressed by many, that the patterns of sublimation revealed in chess and chess players can be generalized into all fields of culture. Is the problem of chess mania the problem of the addicted fanatic or of anyone who plays an occasional game of chess? Surely all activities that become obsessive activities indicate neuroses and, if subjected to analysis, reveal something quite as unpleasant as chess itself.

Of course, the general point is generally true; the *summa* is the psychopathology of everyday life. However, because of its specific form and its social destiny, chess reveals certain patterns with peculiar clarity and force. The amateur, playing the very occasional game, will not be subject to the forces (at least not to the same degree) outlined above. Yet the very hostility with which this author at least has been confronted by outraged enthusiasts, fretful at imagined imputations of homosexuality or masturbatory fantasies, does seem to indicate some basic unease, fairly universal to all players. More difficult to justify is the male-oriented nature of this study and, indeed, of almost all studies of chess. Women have attacked the male domination of the game.[3] Since I have less love for the game than most commentators, I suppose I can risk the response that it can be taken as a creditable sign that women have largely not become involved in chess or as expert as men in its execution, because they are happily without the psychological formations or drives that promote an expertise in the game in the first place. It all depends on your point of view. One could even add that women have never been allowed the cultural space to foster that lethargic, yet zealous commitment to a useless pursuit that has fostered the bizarre careers of the great champions.

Let us now make a brief *tour d'horizon* of these champions. Morphy was not the only one to exhibit eccentricity or indeed to fall prey to paranoia. Fine devotes much of his book to an examination of the other champions of the last hundred years, the better to buttress his conclusions. How do they look?

The chess championship of the world began officially on January 11, 1886, when Wilhelm Steinitz and Johannes Zukertort faced each other at 80 Fifth Avenue in New York City. Steinitz was the victor. Before Steinitz the champions were, unofficially:

Howard Staunton (English)—1844–1851
Adolf Anderssen (German)—1851–1858, 1859–1866
Paul Morphy (American)—1859

since the official birth of the championship:

Wilhelm Steinitz (Austrian)—1886–1894
Emanuel Lasker (German)—1894–1921
José Raul Capablanca (Cuban)—1921–1927
Alexander Alekhine (Russian)—1927–1935, 1937–
    1946
Max Euwe (Dutch)—1935–1937
Michael Botvinnik (Russian)—1946–1957 & 1958–
    1960 & 1961–1963
Mikhail Tal (Russian)—1960–1961
Tigran Petrosian (Russian)—1963–1969
Boris Spassky (Russian)—1969–1972
Robert Fischer (American)—1972–

Excluding Fischer, there are four champions in the history of the game about whom myths have assiduously been built up. Morphy was regarded for a long time as the "greatest player in the history of the game," Steinitz as the "father of modern chess," Capablanca as the "chess machine," and Alekhine as the "greatest attacking player of all time." Needless to say, remarks Fine, such paeans are the fruits of the chess players' addiction to hero worship, but they also remind us of the great champions' own megalomaniac desire for praise and their need for idolatry from their admirers.

The other world champions are the nonheroes. They had other interests apart from chess. Staunton was a Shakespearean scholar (the King of writers). Anderssen was a quiet teacher—chess was his main libidinal outlet and he was above all an attacking player. Lasker had extensive philosophical interests and was an accomplished physicist.

Max Euwe (world champion in the late thirties) is a mathematician—his defect in chess being a tendency to be bowled over by tactical surprises. Botvinnik is an engineer—and he is considered, along with the other Russian champions, later in the book.

This leaves us with the heroes Steinitz, Capablanca, Alekhine and Fischer. Morphy we have already dealt with.

Wilhelm Steinitz came from a very poor family. He became world champion in 1866 and defended the title for twenty-seven years. Eventually he succumbed to Lasker in 1894, when the insecurities of his financial state were beginning to tell on him. Steinitz had tasted scientific procedure during his training to be an engineer, and he employed deductive reasoning in his analysis of chess. The growth of regular match and tournament play in the latter half of the nineteenth century led a trend toward solidity of play and an aversion to hit-or-miss methods. Since many of them were now playing for money, players would seek a more rational basis for attack. Steinitz became one of the first of these entirely professional players, after he rediscovered chess in a Viennese café, having run out of funds as an engineering student.

Edward Lasker writes:

> Before Steinitz, even the greatest chess masters had looked on the game as something in which victory, as a matter of course, would always fall to the one who would conceive the most imaginative plays, and in their games they spent every ounce of their energy on the passionate search for winning combinations. Steinitz was the first to realize that it was idle for a player to expect the gods to send him an ingenious winning idea, unless the strategic plan he followed was based upon correct evaluation on the strong and weak points in the position before him. In other words, he proposed to substitute an objective approach in place of the almost entirely subjective manner in which his contemporaries were playing the game. Nearly all of them, the giants Anderssen, Blackburne, Zukertort and Tchigorin, as well as minor stars such as Gunsberg, Mackenzie, Mason and Winawer, were superior to Steinitz in the conception of complicated combinations. But he defeated them, one after the other, by the irrefutable logic of his reasoning, by leading them on into making attacking combinations in which they had no positional advantages, so that an attack was doomed to failure from the start.[4]

The tragedy for Steinitz was that his scientific, professional approach to the game was not compensated by financial reward on anything more than a minimal level. In 1898, two years before his death, he was still a strong enough player to do well at tournament level, but when asked why he did not step aside and let the younger generation earn some laurels, he replied, "I can spare the fame, but not the prize money."

Steinitz was permanently aggressive. He fought on the chessboard, in the chess columns; he argued endlessly with his friends. He said that his enemies were anti-Semitic, and at one point he started to write a book about Jews in chess. Naturally, Fine adds, such aggression must have gone hand in hand with great anxiety. Indeed Steinitz, as an hysteric, suffered from nervous attacks for much of his life. To try to alleviate nervous tension and insomnia he submitted himself to the Kneip treatment—a form of hydrotherapy that required him to take cold baths.

Steinitz suffered from a brief psychotic episode when he lost the chess championship return match with Lasker in 1896, having already been defeated by him in 1894. Then, as Fine writes:

> after his defeat, he was trying to write his book on Jews in chess as rapidly as possible, and for his purpose hired a young Russian secretary who was fluent in both English and German. He developed a delusion that he could telephone without wire or receiver, and the secretary often found him waiting for an answer from the invisible telephone. He would also go to the window, talk and sing and expect an answer. The secretary reported this to the

American consul, who then suggested that Steinitz
be confined to the Morossow sanitarium. This was on
February 11, 1897. On March 6, 1897, he wrote to a
Viennese physician who was a childhood friend that
"like all lunatics I imagine that the doctors are
crazier than I am." He was also well enough to advise
the psychiatrists: "Treat me like a Jew and kick me
out."

Steinitz was soon released and spent the years that remained to him playing in tournaments. Shortly before
his death in 1900 he once again became the victim of
delusions. He thought that he could emit electrical cur-
rents and thus move the pieces at will. There is a story
that he claimed to be in electrical communication with
God, and that he challenged him to a game, giving him
pawn and move. A few weeks later he died, totally desti-
tute, on Ward's Island.

Although Lasker was not as dramatic a figure as the
heroes I have mentioned, it is worth devoting some
lines to him, not the least reason being that he tends to
be the hero of those who wish the image of the chess
champion to be that of the well-rounded, civilized man,
prey to no dreadful eccentricities or noxious habits. He
was urbane, self-controlled and "a philosopher"—altogether a splendid advertisement for the sport.

By training, Lasker was a mathematician and, unlike
Steinitz, took his degree. He drifted into chess, because,
being a Jew, he was unlikely to obtain a professorship in
a German university. In 1894, at the age of twenty-six,
he beat Steinitz and remained world champion for
twenty-seven years. He was, as befits his general cultural
performance, a well-rounded player, versatile at most

types of play. His philosophical theories as developed out of his obsession with chess do not in fact seem to be quite so urbane as one might expect.

In fact he seems to have proposed, in his book on chess, *Kampf* ("Struggle"), a rather vicious variant of social-Darwinism:

> The struggle that we see in a game of chess is a very refined version of the struggle that goes on among living creatures for domination, for their place in the sun. There is a natural state of greediness, of blind groping at the expense of others. Philosophers have contemplated this brutish mode of existence for centuries; they have yearned for the introduction of universal justice. And what would this universal justice be but the establishment of a Steinitzian equilibrium of forces, of the eternal equality of opposed forces, of a state of frozen immobility.

This is a curious passage for the world chess champion to have written, for he says that universal justice could only be the negation of chess, the cessation of aggression, the end of the game.

It is not surprising, given these sentiments, that he felt he should have no right to a winning position, so long as his opponent had not made any mistakes, or broken rules of strategy or tactics. He thought it almost unethical to try and force a win in a draw game, relying on the hope that the opponent might make a last-minute mistake.

Even with this noble sense of justice and the inevitable, he was all the same an extremely wily player. He would complicate positions to a point where his opponent had to step exceedingly carefully, and he would steer the game into paths that did not suit his opponent's style of play.

In 1908 he married and at the age of forty became, as he put it, husband, father and grandfather in one stroke, since his wife, who was some years older than he, was already a grandmother. In the First World War his principles of universal justice seem somewhat to have abandoned him, and he wrote a book purporting to prove that Germany had to win the war if civilization was to survive. He also invented a kind of tank.

Lasker had little sense of time. He never carried a watch, since he did not want to be enslaved by it. I suppose this was by way of compensating for the fact that during his playing life, Lasker, like all chess players, was tyrannized by time. In a game with Capablanca he insinuated that the Cuban's clock had been specially fixed to run a little slower.

Lasker suffered no dramatic descent into paranoid behavior, beyond the permissible eccentricities associated with the *philosophe* devoted to the things of the mind. In the matter of money he was unlucky. Mindful of the experiences of Steinitz, who died in poverty, he insisted on receiving adequate financial reward in the matches and tournaments in which he participated. He succeeded in this attempt, exacting $10,000 for himself when he played Capablanca in 1921. He saw the whole sum dissipated in the German inflation of 1923. And so, at the age of fifty-three he had to start another, often successful, chess career.

Lasker is interesting not so much on the pathobiographical level as on the sociocultural one. He was, as we have seen, the proudest boast of the chess world, at home not only on the chessboard, but also in the concepts of philosophy and mathematics. Yet for all his powers at the board, his achievements in these other areas were not extraordinary. No one now reads his final work, *The Understanding of the World*; and according to Ernst Cassirer, Lasker was not very familiar with philosophical literature.

As mentioned previously, he saw absolute justice as a situation in which the world was petrified in perfect immobility. How different in spirit from those two socialists, Brecht and Benjamin, who once argued that even the powers of chess pieces should change as the game dialectically developed.[5] Lasker thought also of attacking the problem of free will by purely mathematical induction, another project that should properly have been left on the chessboard, whence its motivation seems to have sprung. Fine tells the story that Lasker criticized Einstein for proposing the theory of relativity without proving that the speed of light in a vacuum is infinite. Einstein replied that one could not wait forever for proof, and he added that Lasker's persistent unwillingness to come to any conclusions came out of his chess-playing temperament, which did not require that anything be settled definitively since, after all, it was only a game. In view of this ambivalence, it is interesting that Lasker's game is the least easy to define.

The two opening variations that bear his name involve an early exchange of Queens—that is, to clarify the situation (his constant ambition in chess), he gets rid of women. He could never finish many of his projects because to do so meant carrying out an aggressive action.

His premature resignation to Capablanca in 1921 may
have been masochistically determined. He finally died
of an illness that could have been cured if he had attended to it earlier.

> Here and there Lasker gives us a glimpse of the pleas-
> ure he derived from the game, a pleasure which is
> consciously denied. Of Tarrasch he once wrote, "He
> lacks the passion that whips the blood." And of his
> celebrated victory over Capablanca at St. Petersburg
> in 1914 he wrote, "The spectators had followed the
> final moves breathlessly. That Black's position was in
> ruins was obvious to the veriest tyro. And now Capa-
> blanca turned over his King. From the several hundred
> spectators there came such applause as I have never
> experienced in all my life as a chess player. It was like
> the wholly spontaneous applause which thunders forth
> in the theater, *of which the individual is almost
> unconscious.*"

Fine italicizes the last few words and adds, "In other
words, at times he could feel that the libidinal satisfaction
in chess was too great." It seems a large deduction to make
from such a phrase. Nonetheless Lasker's public urban-
ity, given a triumphant career in a savagely competitive
game, must have concealed an abundance of less-sanc-
tioned or less generous emotions.

One of the interesting aspects of Capablanca is that,
unlike almost every other chess master, he was very keen
on women. As Edward Lasker recalls, he was rarely up
before lunchtime, and the reasons for his late retirement
were not those of intellectual speculation or chess study.
When he lost to Tarrasch in 1914, it was rumored that

he had sprung straight to the chessboard from the bed of the Grand Duke's mistress. When he lost to Alekhine in 1927 it was thought that he had been up late with dancing girls. Fine remarks that the general excuse for his defeats—philandering—must have received at least his tacit support.[6]

He learned chess as Morphy did—from watching his father play—and like Morphy, he became champion of his home town (Havana) at the age of twelve. He went to Columbia University to study engineering, but soon found himself so good at chess that he abandoned all other studies and took it up full time. At the age of twenty-one he beat Frank Marshall and became champion of the Americas. Unlike other champions, Capablanca was also a rounded gamesman. He played on the Columbia basketball team and was expert at bridge and good at tennis. Nor was he ever placed in the same financial straits as other masters—a fact which no doubt contributed to his equilibrium. In the first place he came from a well-connected family; and after his prowess at chess became evident, the Cuban government gave him a sinecure in its Foreign Office, allowing him to traverse the globe in reasonable comfort.

In a way Capablanca seems to have been the complete sportsman of leisure—a type which has rather gone out of fashion in recent times and was never common at all in the chess world. Like Lasker, he rarely looked at a chess book, relying on his native skill to carry him through every crisis. He was preternaturally calm and seemed to many to have a modest demeanor. He was good at everything that came easily to him. "What did not come easily to Capablanca did not come at all."

His style of play was somewhat in accord with the simple, unalloyed desire to win without undue complication. Fine thinks that his style can be best described as materialistic. Capablanca had only to gain some minor advantage, and then his technique and expertise would suffice. Such a disciplined approach was apparent in his style from the earliest years. "The materialist approach flows directly out of his phallo-narcissistic orientation; win something and the reward follows automatically." He played quickly and therefore had much time for reverie and for dreams.

The land of Cockaigne that Fine mentions refers to a remark in Capablanca's memoirs: "There have been times in my life when I came near to thinking that I could not lose a single game. Then I would be beaten, and the lost game would bring me back from dream land to earth. Nothing is so healthy as a thrashing at the proper time, and from few won games have I learned so much as I have from most of my defeats."

It seems unlikely that Capablanca would have worn his own casual version of private megalomania so lightly if in fact defeats had come more frequently than they actually did. When he entered the New York Masters' Tournament of 1924 he could, as Lasker remarks, "look back on a record that no one had equaled before him and probably no one ever will. He had played ninety-nine tournament and match games in ten years and lost only one!"

The manner in which he bore his losses or contemplated defeat is interesting. There is a story that when he was about to lose a game with Marshall in Havana in 1913 he had the mayor empty the room of spectators before he would admit defeat. Later in his career, on the surface at least, he seems to have been less fragile at the loom of defeat.

Opinions seem to vary about Capablanca. Edward Lasker was much impressed with his personality, finding him alert, well-mannered, with "his obvious feeling of self-confidence tempered by that fundamental modesty which is one of the marks of real intelligence."

Edward Lasker also relates an incident, rare in chess anecdotes, where one player feels pity for another. In a crucial game between Emanuel Lasker and Capablanca in Moscow in 1914, the former suddenly made an error that would probably involve the loss of the game. "Recalling that dramatic moment, Capablanca described how Lasker turned as white as a sheet when he realized his predicament, and how his hands trembled so violently he could hardly grasp the piece he wanted to move. Capablanca never doubted that before long he would be world champion. But, he said, he could not help a feeling of great pity welling up in his heart when he saw the paralyzing effect that the impending defeat had on the aging Lasker. He had held the chess scepter for twenty years and no doubt realized at that moment that his time had come." Actually, Capablanca must have regretted this lack of the killer spirit; Lasker drew that game and eventually finished ahead of Capablanca in the tournament.

However there are other opinions about him. Fine says that he displayed conspicuous arrogance toward men, and that a narrow and somewhat inhuman obsession with victory over his competitors in chess, over women, over everybody was his main motivation.

Rather in keeping with his studiedly casual approach to the game, in the sense that he rarely opened a chess book and rarely played outside tournaments and matches, Capablanca grew bored with chess, and even suggested that the game had ceased to be of interest in its present form. He proposed that the board be enlarged, to admit new pieces, and thus renew and rejuvenate chess.

Altogether, in this as in other aspects, Capablanca was somewhat of an exception to most of the other champions. He enjoyed a secure social position, untroubled by financial care, with his sinecure in the diplomatic service. Although one can see evidence for the narcissism and oral fixation (his keenness on cooking) adduced by Fine, the fact that he did not need to work at chess, owing to his prodigious innate talent, or at a job, because of his sinecure, seems important.

The champion who succeeded Capablanca was as remarkable a character. Alexander Alekhine was the most singular of the chess masters and the one whose life was most clearly marked by his vocation. He was born into a wealthy Russian family in 1892 and was taught the game by his mother at an early age. He played a great deal of blindfold chess at school and became a chess master by the age of sixteen. By 1914 he had already gained his first international success, finishing third to Lasker and Capablanca at St. Petersburg.

With the onset of the Revolution his life became extremely complicated, and there are numerous versions of his movements. Edward Lasker gives the following version:

> When the revolution broke out he served with the intelligence corps of the White Russian Army in

Odessa. The Bolsheviks took the city, and he declared himself "liberated" and acted as a spy for them. When the White Russians recaptured Odessa, Alekhine declared himself liberated again, and he volunteered for counterespionage. Finally the Bolsheviks prevailed, and Alekhine, not too sure that he had succeeded in destroying all damning evidence, summoned all his combinative powers to plot an escape. Under compromising circumstances he practically coerced a young foreign woman to marry him. He thus secured permission to travel abroad. As soon as his train had crossed the Russian frontier, he deserted his wife—and their young son—crudely informing her that he had merely used her for the purpose of getting out of Russia.

There are other legends about him at this period. One of them has it that he was sentenced to death by the Bolsheviks, but was spared by the personal intervention of Trotsky. Another portrays him as responsible for the execution of many White Russians. Ilyin-Zhenevsky, one of the moving forces behind the development of Soviet chess has this account:

> Throughout the period of the war Alekhine served in the Union of Cities [similar to the Red Cross]. The Revolution of 1917 found him doing this work. When the Union of Cities was dissolved, Alekhine, who was a lawyer, became an examining magistrate in the Moscow Criminal Investigation Department. He managed to uncover a number of very involved crimes. His ability to analyze complicated positions in chess helped him in this responsible work. With the passage of time Alekhine, in spite of his noble origins, became more and more pro-Soviet. At the end

> of 1919 or the beginning of 1920 he applied for mem-
> bership of the Communist Party. . . . In 1920 Ale-
> khine left his work in the Moscow C.I.D. and went to
> work in the Communist International. With his mag-
> nificent mastery of foreign languages he worked in the
> Comintern as an interpreter, and at the same time, as
> a Communist, he was appointed secretary to the Ed-
> ucation Department. . . . Early in 1921 Alekhine
> married a foreign Communist, a Comintern delegate,
> and went abroad with her.[7]

It must be remembered, about the latter account, that
although Alekhine was bitterly attacked for many years
in the Soviet press, it would not necessarily have been in
Ilyin-Zhenevsky's interests to have presented him as an
unprincipled ruffian prior to his eventual departure in
1921, since he had not yet fallen prey to noxious foreign
influences. There may have been tactical considerations
too, such as expectations of Alekhine's eventual return.

Alekhine never set foot in Russia again. So far as his
later life is concerned, almost as many rumors are current as about his performance during the Revolution.
Again to quote Lasker:

> Chess was his *only* love. I am sorry to say that in his
> human relations he was governed by utter selfishness
> —even brutality. He concealed these traits carefully
> when he felt that his career might otherwise be ad-
> versely affected. I am recording these facts without
> personal animosity. During the many years of my
> close acquaintance with him we got along very well,
> and I learned of his bad character only much later on.

Fine says simply that he "was the sadist of the chess
world." There are numerous reminiscences of his per-

sonal uncouthness. He drank heavily and turned up drunk for tournaments; he once was discovered lying drunk in a field when he should have been at the board. There is a story that he turned up for one match and urinated on the floor. He was married four more times, after he had abandoned his first *laissez-passer* to the Soviet frontier. At least three of these spouses were twenty-five years older than himself. Fine says he was openly sadistic to his last wife.

There are other, dire charges. "During the war Alekhine became a Nazi collaborator," Fine remarks. "He wrote a series of articles on the 'Aryan' spirit in which he proved that Jews could not play chess, and that they spoiled the purity of the game. Since so many of his colleagues were Jewish, he was boycotted by them after the war." After he had attacked the Soviet Union in a speech to *émigrés* in Paris at the end of the twenties, Ilyin-Zhenevsky wrote, "This speech finally severs Alekhine's ties with the Soviet chess community and places him in the ranks of our irreconcilable enemies."

A Russian chess journal said of him and Bogolyubov, another famous Russian player, in 1934: "Both heroes of the match proved worthy of their hosts [in Nazi Germany]. They clearly understood what was required of them. At fascist meetings, arranged as they traveled from city to city, both villains expressed their whole-hearted support for National Socialism. Alekhine declared that he was ready to sacrifice his life for a Nazi Russia. . . ."

In 1937 Alekhine sent a telegram to Moscow: "With all my heart I congratulate the chess players of the U.S.S.R. on the twentieth anniversary of the October Revolution. Alexander Alekhine." Less than a year later war broke out, and Alekhine found himself associated with the Nazis. During the Second World War he competed in seven tournaments in Germany, and pro-Nazi articles appeared over his signature.

Just after the war Alekhine defended himself to the organizers of the London tournament against charges of collaboration with the Nazis: "For nearly twenty years I have been dubbed a White Russian, which was particularly painful to me, for this made impossible any contact with my native country, which I have never ceased to love and admire."

It seems, on the surface, an unpleasant record. One's impression is that Alekhine conducted his diplomatic relations with a perpetual and unpleasant opportunism, and to judge by the stories about his first wife, this behavior extended to his personal relationships too. One writer reminisces:

> He was a hatchet-faced blond giant, with a sweep of hair over his forehead and several inches of cuff protruding from his sleeve. First, he rests his head in his hands, works his ears into indescribable shapes, clasps his hands under his chin in pitiful supplication, shifts uneasily in his seat like a dog on an anthill, frowns, elevates his eyebrows, rises suddenly and stands behind his chair for a panoramic view of the table, resumes his seat, then, as the twin clock at his side ticks remorselessly on, sweeps his hair back for the thousandth time, shifts a Pawn, taps the clock button and records his move.

He was the most inventive genius the game has had. He lived for chess. In 1927 he beat Capablanca to become world champion and shortly afterward remarked, "You know, a curious struggle takes place within me whenever I play chess. A struggle between fantasy on one side and sheer prudence on the other. You see, too much fancy or too much fantasy is not good. It must be tamed by good, cold sense. The two pull in opposite directions. Yet they must both be gratified. . . . However in my case fantasy dominates. . . . I suppose I'll have to put up with it somehow."

Apropos this urge for fantasy, Lasker remarks: "Alekhine was the very embodiment of the gambler. He delights in making an experiment, curious to see the outcome of it. He would be content to do so forever, delighted to think that his own skill and his own imagination are the cause of all that happens on the board."

Although it is frequently emphasized that the element of chance is absent from chess, and that this absence is one of the game's virtues, the situation is a little more complex than that. Chess players gamble in all sorts of ways. Lasker notes here that Alekhine gambled with new moves. Elsewhere he remarks that some players would never willingly concede defeat, even though the position held no hope, because they were gambling on a faulty move by their opponent. More basically, a player might see a variety of possible moves, each with something to commend them, and eventually trust his luck on one of them. As we shall see, gambling had its place in the early history of chess, in the sense that moves were dictated by throws of dice—and although the modern game excludes such direct appeals to providence, it does not follow that players do not gamble in the course of their reflections. Indeed, one could develop the argument that paradoxically the exclusion of chance, which appears to make chess more serious than other games, actually reduces the reality quotient of the game, not in the trivial sense that history is a chapter of accidents, but in the sense that progress in science and history is largely a matter of understanding, mastering and transcending chance and accident. Chess, by excluding this element from the "raw materials" of the game, as it were, is basically unproductive and idealist. It introduces us to a realm wherein the player is in complete command of his pieces and is pitted absolutely against the subjectivity of his opponent.

Gambling or not, Alekhine had no ability to fall back on Capablanca's phlegmatic comments when he lost a game. He would sometimes hurl his King across the room. On occasion he would smash the furniture. Games generated an enormous tension in him.

Fine detects in him a "strong phallic narcissistic component." Alekhine wanted to destroy his opponents. Alekhine was taught chess by his mother, and Capablanca by his father. Thus, for Alekhine, continued success at chess meant continued involvement with and possession of the mother. Indeed he played chess in bed with his last wife, a great deal older than he. Capablanca, on the other hand, had no allurement and thus finally became bored with chess.

Alekhine's emphasis on attack, Fine remarks, represented a sublimation of the sadistic urges towards the father. Once he had a man down he wanted to destroy him.

This sadism expressed itself markedly in his treatment of Capablanca. After Alekhine's victory over him in

1927, Capablanca was never able to consummate a re-match. When Capablanca accumulated the $10,000 purse needed, Alekhine promptly demanded the equivalent sum in gold. Even in the middle thirties, when Alekhine was certainly Capablanca's superior, the former avoided him, and when Sir John Simon mentioned Capablanca's name during some remarks at a chess tournament in Margate, Alekhine ostentatiously left the room.

Alekhine came from so curious a background and lived such a bizarre life, that his behavior cannot be said to stem from one cause. His father was a member of the nobility and a member of the Duma. This father was also a famous gambler, reputedly having lost a million rubles at one sitting in Monte Carlo. From this background Alekhine was first propelled through the turmoils of the revolution and then into exile. No one country became his home, although he did take out papers as a naturalized French citizen at one point. (On one journey to Warsaw he was stopped at the Polish border for having no papers. He declared, "I am Alekhine, chess champion of the world. I have a cat called Chess. I do not need papers." All these propositions were not necessarily invalid.)

He has been called the last romantic in chess. Certainly, in the vicious and unprincipled zeal with which he pursued his vocation he has some of the attributes of Romantic heroes. His end has also a Bohemian melancholy. He died in 1946, in Portugal. His friend Lupi met him there just before his death and Alekhine remarked, "Lupi, the loneliness is killing me! I must live, I must feel life about me. I have already worn down the floor boards of my room. Take me to some night club . . ."

The last of three heart attacks was fatal, and he was found to have been suffering from arteriosclerosis, chronic gastritis and duodenitis. We might note, incidentally, that Morphy, Alekhine and Capablanca all died of sudden strokes between the ages of forty-five and fifty-five. Fine remarks that this could well be related to the enormous tension under which they lived.We could also speculate that their deaths came, as to so many executives who die several months after retirement, when a successful chess life no longer seemed possible. This is not so true of Morphy, who long before had given up serious chess. But Capablanca had given up hope of once again reaching the front rank by the middle thirties, and Alekhine, with the possibility of being expelled from the International Chess Federation for having collaborated with the Germans, and facing the star of the next generation of Russian players, Botvinnik, had little to look forward to and no other occupation to fall back on.

Before the emergence of Botvinnik as world champion in 1946 there was only one other intervening figure between the two Russians: Max Euwe, who was briefly world champion in 1935. He is the most sedate of all champions. Although he exhibited an early talent for chess he completed his schooling and took his doctorate in mathematics. Chess seems to have been a successful and restrained sublimation. He is a teacher by profession, happily married, with three children. Excluding the Soviet champions, he is the one who has most successfully adapted to ordinary bourgeois life, and who has exhibited least symptoms of oddity.

Surveying the lives of these champions, one must feel

awe at the obsession that carried them forward through life. Champions of any sport practice and perform it, far beyond the limits of normal human enthusiasm. Very rarely does one have this apprehension that such people are pursuing a lifetime vocation, one in which scant financial reward, constant voyaging round the spas and health resorts of the chess world are almost as nothing compared with the constant and insatiable desire to play chess. We do seem closer to the universe of the compulsive gambler (nominally so different) than to the essentially organized and rational procedures of modern professional sport. Such reflections, of course, impinge on the social status of chess and the chess player, and I deal with these later on; but here we can note in passing the truly extraordinary spectacle of Alekhine, for example, savagely uncaring about anything but chess, a pocket set constantly by him, always at work on his art. And not only Alekhine; but Steinitz, Lasker, Capablanca—some of them in the end evident victims of psychoses; all of them for so many years on that leave of absence from reality that is one of the features of play.

Although the champions are not the only chess players to have exhibited strange traits, they are the only ones so far dealt with. There are numerous other players who exhibited neurotic or psychotic features. Fine relates a number of incidents in which we can find symptoms of paranoia, megalomania and exhibitionism. The Mexican master Carlos Torre was, in the middle twenties, regarded as one of the foremost contenders for the world championship. The Mexican government promised him financial aid. Shortly afterward he took off all his clothes on a Fifth Avenue bus, and after hospitalization was returned to Monterrey. There his three brothers looked after him, and he never again left its vicinity.

Torre never slept more than two hours a night and would quite frequently warn his colleagues away from women; they cost too much money, he said. His career, with its pattern of early triumphs, followed by permanent retirement, somewhat resembles Morphy's.

Two other cases of exhibitionism are related by Fine. A Polish master by the name of Frydman is reported to have taken his clothes off during a tournament and rushed through the hotel, shouting "Fire!" And some years ago at a European chess club one of the better players appeared in a large coat that completely enveloped him. He suddenly threw it open to reveal that he was wearing nothing else.

On the matter of exhibitionism, Fine remarks that this phenomenon—and self-exposure—represents an inability to stand the lack of physical contact a moment longer; the subject has to break through the sublimated etiquette of chess and the physical isolation imposed by it, and deploy the real penis, instead of manipulating the symbolic one on the board.

There is one champion absent from this account: Fischer. But before we examine his career and review the accumulated evidence about his personality, substantial detours are necessary. First, another writer's fable about chess and about death; second, the social history of chess, and its career in the country where it has been awarded social respectability in the modern age.

CHAPTER FOUR

Death: Zweig's Last Game

Freud suggests that the aggression in human nature —the drive to master nature as well as the drive to master man—is the result of an extroversion of the death instinct, the desire to die being transformed into the desire to kill, destroy or dominate. . . .

The relation of the pleasure-principle to the Nirvana-principle suggests that man has a history because the balanced equilibrium between tension and release of tension at the animal level has been disrupted and replaced by a dynamic restless striving. The study of the repetition-compulsion suggests that repression generates historical time by generating an instinct-determined fixation to the repressed past, and thus setting in motion a forward-moving dialectic which is at the same time an effort to recover the past. In that perspective on man's historicity the crucial psychoanalytical concept is fixation to the past. In our new perspective the crucial psychoanalytic concept is the repression of death.

—NORMAN O. BROWN: *Life against Death*[1]

"I will never forget," remarked Stefan Zweig in his autobiography, "the sight which once met me in a London travel bureau. It was filled with refugees, almost all Jews, every one of them wanting to go—anywhere. Merely to another country, anywhere, into the polar ice or the scorching sands of the Sahara, only away, only on, because their transit visas had expired and they had to go on, on with wife and child to new stars, to a new language world, to people whom they did not know and who did not want to receive them."[2]

Zweig had seen this travel bureau in 1939—and he wrote those exile's lines in a new language world, in Brazil, just before he committed suicide in 1942. Zweig was a member of that cultivated and brilliant generation of Viennese Jews who reached maturity amid the catastrophe of the First World War and found exile or death with the onset of the Second. As a biographer and short-story writer Zweig's reputation between the wars was immense, though his work and reputation have less meaning today. Jules Romains remarked of him that he was "one of the seven wise men of Europe . . . one of those men whom I have heard oftenest and most regularly say things that were just and wise and human . . ." He was a close friend of Freud, and one of the few *hommes de lettres* who had more than an anecdotal or fashionable acquaintance with his work. His biographical writings were impregnated with Freud's ideas, and the latter regarded Zweig's famous Monte Carlo story as the classic—in psychological terms—exposition of the gambler's psyche.

Like so many of his friends, Zweig fled westward as the Nazis consolidated their power. The year 1939 found him settled in England. But Zweig had to travel "only away, only on." In 1940 he and his wife, Lotte, left for the United States. In 1941 they sailed to Brazil. A year later they both committed suicide, by drugs, in Petrópolis. In his last declaration Zweig remarked that he would gladly have built his life over again in Brazil, "now that the world of my native tongue has perished for me and Europe, my spiritual home is destroying itself. But one would need special powers to begin completely afresh when one has passed one's sixtieth year. And mine have been exhausted by long years of homeless wandering. It seems to me, therefore, better to put an end, in good time and without humiliation, to a life in which intellectual work has always been an unmixed joy and personal freedom earth's most precious possession."

The manuscript of "The Royal Game"[3] reached New York almost coincidentally with the news of the death of his wife and himself. This story about chess was his last piece of writing and the prologue to his own suicide. During its composition Zweig wrote to his friends of the creative hardships involved—and the difficulties he was encountering in writing the story of Dr. B.

As a counterpoint to later dramas, the story begins sedately enough. The narrator is embarking on a ship from New York to Rio de Janeiro. A friend tells him casually that also on board is Mirko Czentowicz, the chess champion of the world. It emerges that Czentowicz has only recently arrived in the chess world. He commenced his existence as a poor peasant in the Banat region of Yugoslavia. Fortuitously he revealed a talent for chess to the local priest, a talent acquired merely by watching his elders play. A local aristocrat sponsors his skill, and in a short time Czentowicz attains the highest ranks in the chess world.

Zweig lays great emphasis on Czentowicz's low mental endowments:

> Thus it occurred that the illustrious gallery of chess masters, which included eminent representatives of widely varied intellectual fields—philosophers, mathematicians, constructive, imaginative and often creative talents—was invaded by a complete outsider, a heavy, taciturn, peasant clod from whom not even the cunningest journalists were ever able to extract a word that would help to make a story. . . . In spite of his correct dress, his fashionable cravat with its too-ostentatious pearl stickpin, and his carefully manicured nails, he remained in manners and behavior the narrow-minded lout who swept the priest's kitchen. He utilized his gifts and his fame to squeeze out all the money they would yield, displaying petty and often vulgar greed, always with a shameless clumsiness that aroused his professional colleagues' ridicule and anger. . . . From the time when he became champion he regarded himself as the most important man in the world, and the consciousness of having beaten all those clever, intellectual, brilliant speakers and writers in their own field and of earning more than they, transformed his early unsureness into a cold and awkwardly flaunted pride.
>
> "There's just one thing in that immured brain of his," remarks a friend to the narrator, "the knowledge that he hasn't lost a game of chess for months, and as he happens not to dream that the world holds other values than chess or money, he has every ground to be infatuated with himself."

The narrator is excited by the news that such a prodigy is on board, and gives vent to a hymn to the game of chess that should, despite its equivocations—which become manifest as the story continues—find a place in every anthology:

> I had never before had the chance to know a great chess player personally, and the more I now sought to familiarize myself with the type, the more incomprehensible seemed a lifelong brain activity that rotated exclusively about a space composed of sixty-four black and white squares. I was well aware from my own experience of the mysterious attraction of the royal game, this one among all games contrived by man which rises superior to the tyranny of chance and which bestows its palms only on mental attainment, or rather on a definite form of mental endowment. But is it not an offensively narrow construction to call chess a game? Is it not a science too, a technique, an art, that sways among these categories as Mahomet's coffin does between heaven and earth, at once a union of all contradictory concepts: primeval, yet ever new; mechanical in operation, yet effective only through the imagination; bounded in geometric space, though boundless in its combinations; ever-developing, yet sterile; thought that leads to nothing; mathematics that produces no result; art without works; architecture without substance, and nevertheless, as proved by evidence, more lasting in its being and presence than all books and achievements; the only game that belongs to all people and all ages and of which none knows the divinity that bestowed it on the world to slay boredom, to sharpen the senses, to exhilarate the spirit. One searches for its beginning and end. Children can learn its simple

rules, duffers succumb to its temptation, yet within this immutable tight square it creates a particular species of master not to be compared with any other —persons destined for chess alone, specific geniuses in whom vision, patience and technique are operative through a distribution no less precisely ordained than in mathematicians, poets, composers, but merely, united on a different level. . . . It stands to reason that so unusual a game, one touched with genius, must create out of itself fitting matadors. This I always knew, but what was difficult and almost impossible to conceive of was the life of a mentally alert person whose world contracts to a narrow, black-and-white one-way street; who seeks ultimate triumphs in the to-and-fro, forward and backward movement of thirty-two pieces; a being who, by a new opening in which the knight is preferred to the pawn, apprehends greatness and the immortality that goes with casual mention in a chess handbook—of a man of spirit who, escaping madness, can unremittingly devote all of his mental energy during ten, twenty, thirty, forty years to the ludicrous effort to corner a wooden king on a wooden board!

Fascinated by the idea of the dumb genius the narrator attempts to attract his attention by playing chess in the ship's saloon. This has no effect, since Czentowicz at once perceives that an amateurish game is in progress, and exhibits no further interest. However, the narrator's chess companion, hearing that the world champion is on board, is at once eager to play him, and by offering him $250 a game gets Czentowicz to agree to play all those interested as a group.

He wins the first game easily. The group are halfway

through their second game, and contemplating a move which they believe to be advantageous, when suddenly one of the players feels his arm gripped. He "heard a voice, low and impetuous, whisper, 'For God's sake! Don't!'"

The narrator sees a man of about forty-five, "whose narrow, sharp face had already arrested my attention on deck strolls because of its extraordinary, almost chalky pallor." The stranger counsels against their move, suggests another course and over the next fifteen moves forces a draw with the champion. "None of us breathed; it had come upon us too abruptly and we were nothing less than frightened in the face of the impossible: that this stranger should have been able to force his will on the world champion in a contest already half lost."

They at once suggest that the stranger play a game with Czentowicz. Haltingly he mutters that this is out of the question; he has not played for twenty-five years. With this news he hurries from the room.

The narrator has perceived that the stranger is Austrian and, as a compatriot, volunteers to try to persuade him to play Czentowicz. Only when pressed with the fact that he has actually forced a draw with the world champion does the stranger reluctantly agree to play, but for motives which only later does he disclose. Dr. B, as he is now described, then tells his story.

Dr. B belonged to an old Austrian family whose business had been the specialized legal one of administering the fortunes of the great monasteries, and of certain members of the imperial family. As soon as the Nazis gained power in Austria, Dr. B was betrayed by a clerk and was arrested. The objective of his interrogators was

to discover the whereabouts of the huge fortunes he has
been tending.

"You might imagine," remarks Dr. B to the narrator,
"that I was thrown into a concentration camp." Nothing
of the sort happened. Like others from whom the Gestapo
hoped to extort millions he was lodged in the Metropole
Hotel.

> A room to oneself in a hotel—sounds pretty decent,
> doesn't it? But you may believe me that they had in
> mind not a decenter but a more crafty technique. . . .
> For the pressure by which they planned to compel
> the needed testimony was to be exerted more subtly
> than through common beating or physical torture—
> by the most complete isolation conceivable. They did
> nothing to us; they merely deposited us in the midst
> of nothing, knowing well that of all things the most
> potent pressure on the soul of man is nothingness.
> . . . There was nothing to do, nothing to hear, noth-
> ing to see; about one, everywhere and without inter-
> ruption there was nothingness, emptiness without
> space or time. One walked to and fro, and with one
> went one's thoughts, to and fro, to and fro, ever
> again. But even thoughts, insubstantial as they seem,
> require an anchorage if they are not to revolve and
> circle around themselves; they too weigh down under
> nothingness. One waited for something from morn to
> eve and nothing happened. Nothing happened. One
> waited, waited, waited; one thought, one thought, one
> thought till one's temples smarted. Nothing hap-
> pened. One remained alone. Alone. Alone.

He is on the verge of breaking down under the strain
of solitude and elaborate interrogation, when suddenly

an event offers him temporary respite. He is waiting for
interrogation one day when he observes "a slight bulge"
in the pocket of one of his jailers. "I moved closer to it
and thought I recognized, by the rectagular shape of the
protrusion, what this swollen pocket harbored: a book!
My knees trembled—a *book!*"

He succeeds in abstracting the book, and manages to
smuggle it back to his room. For a long time he does not
open it. He dreams that "it might be one from which I
could learn and memorize, preferably—oh! what an
audacious dream—Goethe or Homer." Finally the moment comes. With trembling fingers he opens the book.
To his bitter vexation he discovers that it is a chess anthology, a collection of one hundred and fifty championship games.

> Had I not been barred, locked in, I would in my first
> rage have thrown the thing through an open window;
> for what was to be done—what could be done—with
> nonsense of this kind? Like most of the other boys at
> school I had now and then tried my hand at chess to
> kill time. But of what use was this theoretical stuff to
> me? You can't play chess alone, and certainly not
> without chessmen and a board.

Dr. B at first devises a primitive board with the checkered cloth of his bedspread, and pieces out of bits of
bread. In a fortnight he dispenses with this clumsy apparatus.

> The transposition had been accomplished perfectly.
> I had projected the chess board and its figures within
> myself. . . . It cost me no effort, after another fort-

night, to play every game in the book from memory or, in chess language, blind; and only then did I begin to understand the limitless benefaction which my impertinent theft constituted. For I had acquired an occupation—a senseless, a purposeless one, if you wish—yet one that negated the nothingness that enveloped me; the one hundred and fifty championship games equipped me with a weapon against the strangling monotony of space and time.

Soon he discovers that a diet of four games a day from the book is sharpening his wits. He is able to evade his interrogators' traps more easily. He fancies that they are beginning to view him with a certain respect.

Then I arrived unexpectedly at a dead point. Suddenly I found myself once more facing nothingness. For by the time I had played through each one of these games innumerable times, the charm of novelty and surprise was lost, the exciting and stimulating power was exhausted. What purpose did it serve to repeat again and again games whose every move I had long since memorized? No sooner did I make an opening move than the whole thing unraveled of itself; there was no surprise, no tension, no problem. My madness could take but one course: instead of the old games I had to devise new ones myself. I had to try to play the game with myself or, rather, against myself.

But of course, as Dr. B realizes, this is a contradiction in terms of chess.

Such cerebral duality really implies a complete cleavage of the conscious, a lighting up or a dimming of

> the brain function at pleasure as with a switch; in short, to want to play against oneself at chess is about as paradoxical as to want to jump over one's own shadow. . . . The fearful state I was in compelled me at least to attempt this split between Black ego and White ego so as not to be crushed by the horrible nothingness that bore in on me.

So far, Zweig intimates, Dr. B has been telling his story to the narrator in a calm, reflective fashion. At this point he begins to exhibit signs of agitation. His mouth twitches as he travels to the center of his remembered horror.

Dr. B discovers that disaster eventually strikes him, not so much in the auto-cleaving of personality as in the fact that

> with the need to play independently I lost my foothold and fell into a bottomless pit. . . . It was only because the replaying of others' games left my self out of the picture that this activity served to soothe and heal my shattered nerves. . . . From the moment at which I tried to play against myself I began, unconsciously, to challenge myself. Each of my egos, my Black ego and my White ego, had to contest against the other and become the center, each on its own, of an ambition, an impatience to win, to conquer; after each move that I made as Ego Black, I was in a fever of curiosity as to what Ego White would do. Each of my egos felt triumphant when the other made a bad move and likewise suffered chagrin at similar clumsiness of its own.
>
> I was a man seeking an object against which to discharge my long accumulated rage. And as I had nothing else than this insane match with myself, that

rage, that lust for revenge, canalized itself fanatically into the game. Something in me wanted to justify itself, but there was only this other self with which I could wrestle; so that while the game was on, an almost manic excitement waxed in me. . . .

I shall never be able to tell, even approximately, how many games I played against myself during those months in my cell as a result of this crazy insatiability; a thousand perhaps, perhaps more. It was an obsession against which I could not arm myself. . . . The joy for play became a lust for play; the lust for play became a compulsion to play, a phrenetic rage, a mania which saturated not only my waking hours but eventually my sleep too. I could think only in terms of chess, only in chess moves, chess problems; sometimes I would wake with a damp brow and become aware that a game had unconsciously continued in my sleep, and if I dreamed of persons it was exclusively in the moves of the knight, the rook, in the advance and retreat, of the knight's move.

He began to decline physically as well as mentally. "Sometimes I was so weak that when I grasped a glass I could scarcely raise it to my lips, my hand trembled so; but no sooner did the game begin than a mad power seized me; I rushed up and down, up and down with fists clenched, and I would sometimes hear my own voice as through a reddish fog, shouting hoarsely and angrily at myself, 'Check!' or 'Mate!' "

Dr. B suffered a complete collapse. He attacked a warder, gashed his arm badly on a window and was taken to a hospital. During his incarceration Bohemia had been occupied, and thus his own importance in the eyes of the Gestapo had been nullified. He had merely to leave the country within a fortnight. Only on the ship to South America has he had time, after the business of actual departure, to review his experiences. The sight of people playing chess against one another with real pieces had come as a shock to him. And now he agrees to play for only one reason: "what interests and fascinates me is nothing but the posthumous curiosity to see whether what went on in my cell was chess or madness, whether I was already at the dangerous brink, or already beyond it—that's all, nothing else."

Dr. B makes only one reservation. He will play just one game—"The idea is merely to close an old account, a final settlement, not a new beginning . . . I cannot afford to sink back a second time into that passionate play fever that I recall with nothing but horror."

The following day the great game takes place. Czentowicz remains immobile as a block the entire time; "thinking seemed to cost him almost physical effort that called for extreme concentration on the part of every organ."

Dr. B "on the other hand, was completely slack and unconstrained. Like the true dilettante, in the best sense of the word, to whom only the play in play—the *diletto* —gives joy, he relaxed fully."

But the narrator soon notes with alarm that Dr. B is already exhibiting agitation. He gulps down glass after glass of tonic water. He begins to pace the salon faster and faster, never deviating from a uniform span. The narrator realizes with a shudder that it is an unconscious reproduction of the pacing in his erstwhile cell. "It must have been like this that he pelted forward and back a thousand times there, the red lights of madness in his paralyzed though feverish state."

Suddenly, after a triumphant move by Dr. B, it becomes apparent that a crisis in the game has been reached. And after a ten-minute pause Czentowicz sweeps the pieces from the board. He has resigned.

Czentowicz loses no time in challenging Dr. B to another game. Despite the warnings of the narrator, Dr. B agrees at once. A new element enters the contest, "a dangerous tension, a passionate hate. No longer were they two players in a sporting way; they were two enemies sworn to destroy each other." Czentowicz plays deliberately slowly; Dr. B becomes at first visibly excited and then strangely abstracted. The narrator realizes that he is playing other games in his head. "My conviction grew that he had really forgotten all about Czentowicz and the rest of us in this cold aspect of his insanity, which might at any instant discharge itself violently."

Suddenly Dr. B pushes his bishop forward and shouts loudly, "Check! Check, the King!" Czentowicz looks up with "a scornful and satisfied smile." He is not in check. Dr. B has been playing an entirely imaginary game on the board. The hard grip of the narrator on Dr. B's arm finally restores him to reality. At once he apologizes. "Forgive the disgrace. It is the last time I yield to the temptation of chess."

"He bowed and left," concludes the narrator, "in the same modest and mysterious manner in which he first appeared before us. I alone knew why this man would never again touch a chessboard, while the others, a bit confused, stood around with that vague feeling of having narrowly escaped something uncomfortable and dangerous."

This little masterpiece of equivocation and despair is like a game itself. It is as if the whole story is an expansion of one of the key phrases in it—"to and fro, to and fro." Zweig's meditation on culture, on contest, on games, on time, on solitude is so perfectly balanced, that only with the finale, as Dr. B rushes from the salon, do we realize that a crisis has been reached, and not resolved.

The hero, if you will, is culture—the universe in which the narrator and Dr. B have always moved. What Zweig does is to confront this culture with its opposite: emptiness, meaningless diversion, barbarism. For much of the narrative the confrontation is never direct: it is built up by implication and by irony. But those who might argue that chess is merely a mechanism in the tale to assist in this confrontation would miss the point. The game is a main participant, and Zweig's final assessment of its meaning is by no means a friendly one.

The first of the equivocations, or ambiguities, comes in the presentation of Czentowicz and the game of which he is the foremost exponent. Czentowicz is a dolt; his only interest exterior to the game is money. He lacks the facility of mental projection: he cannot visualize a chessboard; he has to have the solid pieces before him. As if to underline the contrast, the narrator launches into a rapturous flight on the game itself—"this one among all games contrived by man which rises superior to the tyranny of chance and which bestows its palms only on mental attainment—" but at once he adds a qualifier—"or rather on a definite form of mental endowment." He compounds this qualification in a series of antitheses: ". . . ever developing, yet sterile; thought that leads to nothing; mathematics that produces no result; art without works; architecture without substance, and nevertheless, as proved by evidence, more lasting in its being and presence than all books and achievements. . . ." On a deeper level Czentowicz is, for Zweig, clearly a symbol of the Nazi plague sweeping Europe.

Zweig again returns to the virtues of the game: that it can slay boredom and sharpen the senses. But it produces a particular species of master, not to be compared with any other . . . fitting matadors. Then he poses the final puzzle: could one conceive of a "mentally alert person . . . of a man of spirit who, escaping madness can unremittingly devote all of his mental energy during ten, twenty, thirty, forty years to the ludicrous effort to corner a wooden king on a wooden board!"

Now these questions are staples of any meditation on chess: the expense of prodigious energy on a "meaningless" activity; the nature of chess talent and chess addiction.

By a series of strategies Zweig heightens such leisurely speculation into a series of burning questions. First of all, he counterposes an imbecile with a talent, the "fitting matador," with a cultivated representative from his own background, the Viennese middle classes. Secondly, he confiscates Dr. B's culture. We should not take lightly the speed with which Dr. B finds himself going mad in his hotel room, once bereft of conversation and books. In a matter of days he is disoriented, almost at the mercy of his interrogators, moving to and fro in his cell, an involuntary chess piece himself. Culture is the measured manipulation of time, a tactic for consuming it with a good conscience. Dr. B is no longer in command of time; he is its prisoner.

For a moment of wild hope, after he has stolen the book, he imagines that he has in his hands an intimation of his real world, the world of Homer and Goethe. After a moment's despair he takes the "cultured" attitude on chess, and it seems to offer him the consolation the cultured world expects of chess. He becomes alert again; he can parry his interrogators' questions. So far he is in command of his "leisure" and his time. He allots himself four games a day and feels much the better for his play activity.

But we are still within the bounds of the rational and the relaxed. Dr. B is only miming the game, copying the combinations of the masters. But "suddenly I found myself once more facing nothingness." Zweig returns again and again to this void. This time Dr. B really has to commit himself to the only counterweight to nothingness that he has available. He is no longer master of the game; it masters him. It consumes his thoughts, and wastes his body—"the joy for play became a lust for play; the lust for play became a compulsion to play, a phrenetic rage, a mania . . ." His time, which he had briefly rescued from his jailers by playing with it, once again is confiscated; game time becomes prison time, but now entirely internalized; he has become his own jailer.

We are reminded of the narrator's question at the start: Can a man of spirit, escaping madness, devote himself to the chessboard? We have now one answer in the insanity of Dr. B. But it is only an interim one, for he had been denied one of the essential elements of play—

the capacity to submit oneself voluntarily to the rules and time span of the game.

Zweig resets the scene on the ship. This time Dr. B can volunteer to play. At first we seem to have an optimistic conclusion. A man of spirit and culture can defeat the world champion. But this is only a temporary consolation. In the contest with Czentowicz, Dr. B is described as the traditional games player in the humanist tradition—"Like the true dilettante in the best sense of the word, to whom only the play in play—the *diletto*—gives joy, he relaxed fully." How different a picture from the one Dr. B has given of himself to the narrator, when describing his descent to madness in the hotel—"It goes without saying that I am now fully aware that this state of mine was nothing less than a pathological form of overwrought mind for which I can find no other name than one not yet known to medical annals: chess poisoning."

But the *diletto* cannot for long maintain this poise. Halfway through the second game he suffers a relapse. He cannot escape madness, and hence cannot avoid defeat. The brute wins.

In Zweig's description of the chess games there is an element that should not be missed: the theme of aggression. Zweig plays with this, rather as he plays with the idea of time. Dr. B, lodged in the cultural universe of Goethe and Homer, is of the least aggressive of men. He is quite explicit that there is a strong masochistic element in his struggle—as well as the violent desire to revenge himself on his captors. But even when the battlefield is transferred from a lodging entirely within Dr. B's head to the board placed between himself and Czentowicz, the aggression continues. There is "passionate hate. No longer were they two players in a sporting way: they were two enemies sworn to destroy each other."

Once again, it is Dr. B who is destroyed.

Like Dr. B, Zweig sailed to a new life in South America. The "Royal Game" was his envoi. Why should he have expended his final creative efforts on such a story? The answer must be that he wanted to write a parable of despair and emptiness.

He submits his cultural standards to a series of bitter distortions. He takes a game, the game of games, one which is the supreme endorsement of mind and not providence, and shows there is a tug at its center that leads not to stability, but to madness; the talent that survives this pull belongs to a man who symbolizes, not the cultural glories of Europe, but the sensibility of the brutes who are destroying it.

He takes a cultured man and shows how little it takes to destroy him—not the concentration camp, but the bare room bereft of books.

Above all, he takes the idea of "play activity," the relaxing suburb of cultural activity, and shows that this is no suburb, but a quite different terrain. Time need no longer be a servant; it is a master. Recreation can become a dreadful penance. Playful aggression can become madness. The wooden board and the wooden king become not the pleasant adornments of a book-lined study, but symbols of a world Zweig was happy to leave in Petrópolis.

Three fictions about chess, three deaths. Luzhin leaps from his window, committing, according to Nabokov, *sui mate*. Morphy, in Miss Keyes's final chapter entitled "Shah-Mat," overturns his chess table and then dies in his bath. Dr. B, we may assume, has not long to live. But these are fictions. Is it fair to extract from them the implication that chess has more than a coincidental relationship with death? Medieval iconography saw the relationship. It was death that said Check Mate. And there are many intimations, in all treatments of the game above the purely technical, that establish the same alliance.

The late works of Freud are notorious for inspiring vapid speculation. Yet it seems to me that the implications of some of these later works do something to resolve the chess enigma. One of the most stimulating guides is Norman Brown, whose *Life against Death*[4] has certainly been the most influential of recent extrapolations and developments of the late Freud.

Initially then, I will synopsize Brown's expansion of Freud's views on the death instinct. *Firstly*, "biological and psychological considerations suggested that the activity of all organisms and also of the human mind was directed at getting rid of tensions and attaining inactivity." But the pleasure principle is the search for a quality of experience that repressed consciousness does not afford. It is active, discontented. But if the basic design of man is to attain equilibrium and end repression, then the active pleasure principle returns to the Nirvana principle, moving from anxious quest to repose. What Brown calls "the full life" is the equilibrium between the pleasure principle that belongs to Eros and the Nirvana principle that "belongs to the Death instincts." In this equilibrium life would be a tranquil affirmation, outside history, since "the restless pleasure principle—which is the morbid manifestation of the Nirvana principle—is what makes man Faustian and Faustian man is history-making man."

Secondly, Freud contrasted with the pleasure principle the repetition compulsion, "that compulsion to repeat which in many cases produces fixations to traumatic experiences in the past and a daemonic compulsion to bring suffering on oneself." Brown puts it most eloquently:

> Man, the discontented animal, unconsciously seeking the life proper to his species, is man in history; repression and the repetition compulsion generate historical time. Repression transforms the timeless instinctual compulsion to repeat into the forward-moving dialectic of neurosis which is history; history is a forward-moving *recherche du temps perdu*, with the repetition compulsion guaranteeing the historical law of the slow return of the repressed. And conversely, life not repressed—organic life below man and human life if repression were overcome—is not in historical time. If we connect—as Freud did not—the repetition compulsion with Freud's reiterated theorem that the instinctual processes in the id are timeless, then only repressed life is in time, and unrepressed life would be timeless or in eternity. . . . The Sabbath of Eternity, that time when time no more shall be, is an image of that state which is the ultimate goal of the repetition compulsion in the timeless id.

Thus, the repetition compulsion is a quest for equilibrium, but is always agitated, caught between History and the Sabbath of eternity when history is abolished.

Time, in this perspective, is a psychological problem. Our comprehension of time is a function of our neuroses and our repression. Beyond, in the universe explored by poets, mystics and philosophers there is an absolute non-time. Time schemes for humanity are strictly relative. Time has a different function for animals than for man. In animals the repetition compulsion is evidently a biological tendency, a definition of the creature's limits and behavior, a delineation of psychic and physical territory. The parameters of the repetition represent the *ne plus ultra* of its nature and behavior. But in man this repetition compulsion becomes "a regressive fixation with the past" which is at the same time neurotically dynamic, since this fixation with the past compels man on a search of what he might become. But if man could only rediscover equilibrium, if repression could be overcome, then "the regressive fixation to the past would dissolve; the restless quest for novelty would be reabsorbed into the desire for pleasurable repetition; the desire to *become* would be reabsorbed into the desire to *be*."

Now, as Brown points out, the Nirvana principle and the repetition compulsion are both ways of stating a human objective, which is the instinctual demand for complete satisfaction and the abolition of repression. But why does Freud insist on the idea of the death instinct? What have the Nirvana principle and the repetition compulsion got to do with death?

This brings us to the *third* component of Freud's death instinct: the sadomasochistic complex. Man can love and man can hate; "for Freud as for Saint Augustine mankind's destiny is a departure from, and an effort to regain paradise. In between these two terms man is at war with himself—driven, says Saint Augustine, by two loves, true love on the one hand and the lust for power (*libido dominandi*) on the other." Psychoanalytic terms propose this conflict on the instinctual level in a duality of Eros and the aggressive instinct. Psychoanalysis always qualifies the idea of aggression, seeing it as capable of being turned inward as of being directed outward, as overt intention masking true intention. Which comes first, sadism or masochism? "Aggression turned inward on the self in the form of self-destruction would be a death instinct."

Man cannot face death directly, without anxiety, as the natural counterpart to life. "Under conditions of general repression the death instinct operates malignantly."

Such are the general terms of Brown's development of Freud: the tension between the pleasure principle and the Nirvana principle; the tension between neurotic activity and repose; the repetition compulsion, which is a restless fixation that runs only to seek rest; the desire to hurt, which is self-mortification. All are personae in the Dance of Death.

Can one see in games a mime of the drama described above? Why should we not take chess as a paradigm of these patterns? Do we not find in it "the restless pleasure principle which is the morbid manifestation of the Nirvana principle." All games addicts know the tension in the execution of the game which is pitted against the desire for resolution, for victorious tranquillity, "a balanced equilibrium between tension and tension release" which is never satisfactorily realized.

In the unending plays and replays of old moves and

old patterns a form of the repetition compulsion is taking place. In the symbolism of the chessboard the player shows—to repeat the quotation—"that compulsion to repeat which in many cases produces fixations to traumatic experiences in the past and a daemonic compulsion to bring suffering on oneself." The repetition compulsion is neurotic and endless, localized and enhanced on the chessboard. And, of course, the aggressive instinct is allowed full deployment on the board, in the form of the burning desire to vanquish the opponent, in a reversal of masochistic urges.

We are the victims of an insipid humanism if we see in games only man's better self, released from care into cultural sport. The spectacle of games should induce in us not always uplifting hope, but despair at the sterile rituals in progress, where the participants restlessly seek a tranquillity which, no sooner satisfied, is reborn in the desire for further struggle, still sterile, never satisfied. Games become a strange parody of our existence, an ironic emblem of neurotic vanity.

Zweig called chess "ever developing yet sterile; thought that leads to nothing." It may have been a final irony for Zweig, conversant as he was with Freud's writings, that the game played out by his hero against that symbol of Fascism, Czentowicz, was burdened with such implications. It was an elaborate metaphor for the onset of darkness; but, given Zweig's suicide at Petrópolis, it seems permissible to suppose that its author understood the true meaning of his story. Chess for him meant death.

It is a paradox that the Royal Game should be amenable to such interpretation, because people do not conventionally associate games with death. But those who counter that chess is simply "a war game" should pause to consider what this implies; and while they propose with complacency that chess is the "game of games," they should reflect on why this is so, and whether it is so because chess is the supreme playful intimation of mortality and intimation of the death to come, and the death we flee from, yet desire.

CHAPTER FIVE

Downward Mobility: The Social History of a Game

It seems difficult to deny that the approach of Jones and Fine, and the pathobiography of some players over the last hundred years, do much to "explain" the game. There have been other types of approach: the philosophical essays of writers like Emanuel Lasker; the studies of the academic psychologists, who concentrate on the kind of intelligence required to play the game well and on the thought processes a player will employ during the game. Such inquiries have extended to consideration of the prodigy and to attempts to divine the nature of infantile talent.[1] Latterly there have been numerous studies of the possibilities of computer chess, and what such possibilities tell us about computers and about the human brain.[2] And naturally there is the immense body of instructional manuals, technical histories of the game, compilations of games played. This is the kind of study favored largely by chess players, who seem to seek a strictly functional utility in their literature.

What follows is an attempt to sketch out a social history of chess, following it through its career from origins bathed in myth to a high summer of aristocratic popularity in the Middle Ages, to its increasing separation into an amateur and a "professional" vocation, to its status in the present day. As I have remarked earlier, isolated reading of the purely psychoanalytic texts, without consideration of the *social position* of chess can promote an inadequate understanding of the game and its leading representatives.

To anyone who contemplates the sedate procedures of the game today some of the stories of its conduct in the past will come as a surprise. Great violence often attended chess in its early days. In many of the stories it is the center of battles, murders and in one instance actual castration. But, says Norman Reider, whose essay in the structural analysis of the myths surrounding the origins of chess is of great interest, "all this violence and love have slowly dwindled away, as the game has become a democratic one: it has been sublimated into a mathematical science with a somewhat masculine, homosexual flavour."[3]

Chess has never remained in a state of immobility, locked into the same social set and confined within the same rituals. Today it has a somewhat ambivalent social position; it is not merely sanctioned as play (and occasionally promoted as a spectacle) and as "time off" from other meaningful social activity. It is also regarded as an art, as something strange but estimable. But the professional, or permanently addicted player is not usually regarded as a "socially useful" person—except in the U.S.S.R., which I will discuss in the next chapter—but rather as one dedicated to another nonproductive, socially meaningless world. He is either always searching for perfection, the pure but useless solution to the chess "problem" and never finding it, or he may find it, in which case he has solved something. But what? In our world his achievement has no meaning beyond itself. Thus, at the same time as the *play* of the chess enthusiast is conditioned by all the pressures outlined in earlier chapters, his actual social existence is also compromised by questions about its utility and purpose. Thus are the psychological pressures compounded.

Yet in earlier times it would not have been possible to detect the equivalent pressures—because the whole social set of play was different, and because the game itself had different and richer meanings.

[1]

Firstly let us review the myths about the origins of chess, and what they tell us about the psychological forces the game symbolized or generated:

> Chess is unique among games in that its origin has been the subject of so much creative imagination, made attractive, I believe, because the family romance of the game in conjunction with its artistic character lends itself as a ready vehicle for diplacement on to it of elements of psychic conflicts. Moreover the mystery of the actual origin of the game adds impetus to its use in myths.[4]

No fewer than twenty-four legends about the origins of chess can be gleaned from the authorities on the subject. The themes can be classified as follows: (a) father murder, with chess as the therapeutic agent; (b) chess as a preparation for war; (c) chess as a substitute for war; (d) chess as a diversion; (e) chess as an intellectual struggle; (f) chess as an educative process for morality; (g) the *mater dolorosa* theme. Reider considers the myths from the point of view of their inherent motivations, rather than in chronological terms or from analysis of their cultural origins.

There are two European legends that contain the unembellished theme of father murder. Both of them date from the thirteenth century.[5] In the first, an Eastern philosopher invents the game in the reign of Evil Merodach, regularly presented in the Middle Ages as a monstrous sadist. Evil Merodach chopped up the body of his father Nebuchadnezzar into three hundred pieces and threw them to three hundred vultures. Wise men then invented chess to cure him of his madness. The other version of this story has a philosopher called Justus inventing chess in order to reform a tyrant, Juvenilis. In both these stories the son murders his father and a wise man invents the game as therapy. As Reider emphasizes, the cure is a disguised version of the crime—the murderer repeats in game the traumatic act. The other important point is that the player is also defending his own King against the attacks of his opponent; thus he salves his conscience. Chess is a matter of both father murder and attempts to prevent it.[6] This mirror function of chess is of extreme importance; obviously the player appears both in a monstrous and in a virtuous capacity—planning parricide, at the same time warding it off; recreating Oedipal fantasy, yet trying to disrupt it. Yet the stronger urge is the monstrous one; the player wants to win, to kill the father rather than defend him, although one could clearly speculate on the problems of players who habitually lose at the last, or fail to clinch the expected victory. Reverting to the myths, it is difficult to explain why the theme of father murder was stated so explicitly in medieval literature, whereas in earlier legends it is dealt with more covertly. One explanation, part and parcel of some of the historical theses advanced below, is that such stories coincide with the rise of the absolutist monarch.

In his ordering of the myths in various categories, Reider has them expanding from the central theme of parricide; thus he hypothesizes, even if he cannot prove, that "when chess is clearly intended to be a military substitute the psychological equating of patricide and war is a valid one." So, he has the next group of legends as being "derivative of the aggressive part of the Oedipal theme (i.e. a displaced image of father murder)." Such legends portray chess as a preparation for war. Thus, as-Safadi says: "It is told that when Sissa had invented chess and produced it for King Shihram the latter was filled with amazement and joy. He ordered that it should be preserved in the temples and held it the best thing he knew as a training in the art of war, a glory to religion and the world, and the foundation of all justice."[7] In the next group of legends chess becomes a substitute for war: "a certain King of India, peaceably inclined, procured the invention of chess in order that his fellow monarchs might settle their disputes over the board without effusion of blood."[8]

A natural development of this theme is the notion that chess was invented as a diversion from war. In one such story a king, passionately fond of war, has overcome all his enemies and is bored and ill. A sage, instructed to distract him, invents chess: "The king tried the game, ascertained that the philosopher spoke truly, and found distraction and health in playing chess."[9]

Myths about the origins of chess as associated with an intellectual struggle are usually expressed in the triumph of chess over dice games, such as backgammon. Now, although it is true that chess, in its earliest manifestations, could be played with a die that dictated the moves (a procedure that continued as an option open to players as late as the twelfth century), there are a number of myths which express the opposition between ratiocination and providence. The account in Murray's *History of Chess* is fascinating:

> Several legends connect the invention of chess in some way or other with the game of nard (tables, backgammon). . . . This linking of two games that to us seem so dissimilar—chess, a game in which chance plays the smallest of parts, and nard, a game in which chance plays the dominant part—appears somewhat singular, yet no association of games has been so persistent or has endured so long. It was not only prominent in Muslim lands, where it runs through all the legal discussion, the literature and the traditions, but even in Christian Europe chess and tables appear in constant juxtaposition. The player of chess appears almost everywhere in the literature of the Middle Ages as a player of tables also. . . . In Muslim literature it is upon the essential difference between chess as the game of skill and nard as the game of chance that stress is everywhere laid. The player's complete liberty to select the move he wished

to make in chess is contrasted with the player's sub-
jugation to the dominion of blind chance in nard.

So, al-Mas'udi, a Muslim scholar writes:

> It was at this time that nard and its rules were in-
> vented. It is symbolical of property, which is not the
> reward of intelligence or strength in this world, just
> as possessions are not gained by scheming. . . . The
> two dice represent fate and its capricious dealings
> with men. The player, when the chances are favour-
> able, secures what he wants; but the ready and pru-
> dent man cannot succeed in gaining what a happy
> chance has given to the other. Thus it is that property
> is due in this world to a fortunate chance. The next
> King was Balhait. At this time chess was invented,
> which the King preferred to nard, because in this
> game skill always succeeds against ignorance. . . .
> The game of chess became a school of government
> and defence; it was consulted in time of war, when
> military tactics were about to be employed, to study
> the more or less rapid movement of troops. . . .[10]

The same book by al-Mas'udi quotes the pithy thought
of a Muslim philosopher that the inventor of chess was a
believer in free will, while the inventor of nard was a
fatalist who wished to show by this game that man can
do nothing against fate, and that the true wisdom is to
mold one's life in agreement with the decrees of chance.[11]

Many of the treatises on chess and its multiplicity of
possible developments tell the story of the reward chosen
by the philosopher who thought up the game. The king
who had ordered the search for a new diversion was
taught to play the game and promptly offered the philosopher any reward he chose. The latter asked that he

be given the quantity of wheat that would result from the placing of a single grain on the first square of the chessboard and, on each of the other sixty-three squares in turn, doubling the number of grains allotted to the preceding square. The king readily agreed to this, then soon discovered that the amount demanded was impossibly large. According to the Muslim writer, "the Indians ascribe a mysterious interpretation to the doubling of the squares of the chessboard; they establish a connection between the First Cause which soars above the spheres and on which everything depends, and the sum of the quantities on the 64 squares. This number equals 18,446,744,073,709,551,615 [a quantity of grains, which would apparently cover England to a depth of 38.4 feet]. The Indians explain by these calculations the march of time and of the ages, the higher influences which govern the world, and the bonds that link them to the human soul." It is difficult, at this distance from the time, to see why, but no doubt $2^{64} - 1$ could express a great deal.

Reider comments on this group of stories:

> In this ending to many of the legends of chess we see a return of the repressed, a return of the magical influence. I feel that the story of the reward repeats the theme of the origin of chess, in that the wise man vanquishes the king and proves superior to him, thereby representing the superiority of the intellect over might and force. It is another derivative of the Oedipal situation, a derivative of the cultural trends which betray the ambivalence to royalty, the father-figure—pleasing him on the one hand and impoverishing him on the other. . . . Viewed in terms of psychoanalytic theory the invention of chess ex-

pressed the triumph of secondary-process thinking over the primary process.

It is not really necessary here to lay such stress on the Oedipal connection: the idea of fooling the king with a numerical trap is certainly one that would amuse Muslim scholars, conscious of their own dignity and superior intelligence.

Finally we come to the legends associated with the *mater dolorosa*, or "grieving mother." The two earliest legends concerning the origin of chess both have this theme. One, recorded in the first century of Islam tells of a queen-prophetess whose favorite son was killed by a rebel. The men of her kingdom tried to prevent her from learning of his sad fate, for they feared her reaction. They went to a philosopher, Qaflan, for counsel. After three days' thought he summoned a carpenter, who fashioned him a chessboard according to his direction. Then he invented the game with the remark, "This is war without bloodshed." The news of the invention was permitted to reach the queen, who then asked to see the philosopher and his invention. "He called his disciple, and they played before the queen, and the winner said 'Shah Mat,' and she remembered and knew what he wished her to know, and she said, 'My son is dead.' "

A slightly later version of the same story had the queen's two sons, each by a separate marriage, quarrel and finally resort to war. One died in battle, and when the news came to the queen, she accused the brother of murder. He could not satisfactorily explain to his mother how the death happened, and so he called together the wise men of his kingdom and laid his case before them.

They invented the game of chess and made clear how a king can fall in battle without having been slain. The son then took his game of chess to his mother and thus explained the death of his brother. She continued to study the board all that day and night without desiring food until death released her from her sorrow—"and from that time the chessboard has remained in the knowledge of all mankind."

The curious element in these two very early legends is that the central figure is a queen. Now, the Queen piece was not introduced on the chessboard, as we shall see shortly, until the end of the Middle Ages. But the early Muslim scholars, whose literature has little mention of women, did not hesitate to put them into the legends. Reider speculates that the importance of the queen mother in these stories is a relic of matriarchal myths. It is interesting that game followed myth, after a long time lapse, and the pieces on the board finally fully enacted the Oedipal drama.

Thus the legends contain in them myths of patriarchal and matriarchal settings, of bipolar or Oedipal character, in which the drama of the son's murder of the father, and even of the mother's intentional participation in, or acquiescence to, the deed is enacted. From the earliest days, writers about chess saw in it elements of the family romance. "The theme of father murder is not the only one which is enacted, but many derivatives of the family situation, including denials of the general theme of patricide." Reider concludes his study "Chess, Oedipus and the Mater Dolorosa" with this reflection:

> Thus it appears that the fascination of the game may very well depend in part on the fact that its devotees

experience, sometimes with full measure of affect, the passions and mysteries of the unconscious. These break through the defensive intellectual formalism and structure and add to the pleasure of the game. It is as if, in the enjoyment of the game, one experiences a kind of *unio mystica* with kings and queens, with their family romance, and in participating in its royal richness, a part of lost omnipotence is recaptured.

[2]

Today, with the two, usually male, players sitting silently opposite each other, rigidly controlled in their etiquette, little of the dramatic richness of the conduct of the game in older times remains. Very different was the atmosphere in which it was played and the terms in which it was discussed when it first arrived in western Europe.[12] Many stories about the game in the late Middle Ages carry ample reference to physical battles between opponents, murder and, on one occasion, castration. Although the Church frowned on the game when it first became popular in Europe in the eleventh and twelfth centuries, later ecclesiastical lawyers went to the opposite extreme. Not only was it declared legal to play at chess, but if a clerk quarreled with an opponent and killed him, it was accounted a casual and not a deliberate homicide. There are really two sets of reasons for the greater color of the game at this period: one is that the game had a more ample social function and status; the other is that its symbolism was extremely attractive to medieval moralists.[13]

During the latter part of the Middle Ages, remarks H. J. R. Murray, the greatest historian of chess, and especially from the thirteenth to the fifteenth century, chess in western Europe attained a popularity that has never been excelled and probably never equaled at any later date. By 1250 the early prejudice of the Church against chess had begun to weaken in view of the noble and royal patronage of the game, and the monastic orders were freely accepting chess as a welcome alleviation of monotony, while a knowledge of chess had spread downward from the inmates of castle and monastery to the wealthier burgesses and merchants of the towns. It was played by the Jews in the ghettos. It was an essential portion of the expertises of the troubadour or minstrel that he should be a chess player, and he carried the implements of play with him.

In reputation, though, chess was mainly a game of the upper classes. It is mentioned again and again in literature as one of the typical pastimes of the feudal nobility. Henry I allowed his brother, Robert, Duke of Normandy to play chess during his imprisonment. Ricardus de Camino was murdered in 1312 "while, as nobles do, he was playing chess to keep his spirits up." King James I was playing chess when his murderers burst in on him in 1437. If it was desirable to add color to a romance in which a noble was concerned, a useful trick was to have him playing chess; and this often occurred in real life. King John was playing chess when the deputies from Rouen arrived in 1213 to ask for his help against Philip Augustus, who was besieging the city. Conradin was playing chess when his imminent execution was announced to him in 1268. Chess incidents formed an important part in the development of many medieval romances. In *Lancelot*, for example, the hero is shown a magic chessboard by a lady who tells him that, however well he can play, the pieces will mate him in the angle of the board.[14] In a Dutch version of the Gawain tale the hero comes to a castle in which a hall is arranged as a chessboard, on which chessmen of life size move when touched with a magic ring.

The acquisition of a knowledge of chess and tables formed a considerable part of the education of a nobleman's children, and there are several instances in the romances of children playing chess and quarreling over their games. Skill in play was reckoned as one of the knightly accomplishments. The game was not confined to the male sex; the noble's daughter learned the game alongside her brother and grew up as fond of the game and as proficient at it as any man. Queen Guinevere is described as being a player of the highest skill.

Men did not always take their defeats well. When Jeanne, daughter of Baldwin IX, Count of Flanders, beat her husband he retaliated with his fists. In revenge she left him in captivity from 1213 to 1226, refusing to ransom him. There is an even more intimidating tale, with rich overtones. According to Walter Map, two Breton nobles had quarreled, and one had mutilated the other. The King of France patched up the quarrel by marrying the son and daughter of the two contestants. One day the pair were playing chess, when the husband was called away. A knight took his place and was mated by the lady, who said pointedly, "Mate! Not to you, but to the lordly son." When the husband heard of this he went off and treated his wife's father in the same way as his father had been treated, and returned home with the members of which he had deprived his victim. He called for a chessboard and as he won he threw the members on the table, saying "Mate! To the lordly daughter."

Not all encounters were so savage. The sexes met in equality over the board, and it was indeed a device to permit association of the sexes. It was even permissible to visit a lady's chamber to play chess with her. Lancelot visited Guinevere, under the pretext of playing chess with her; in another story, Beatrix had fallen in love with Bernier. He was tormented with shyness, and she invited him to come to her room to play chess or tables, and find his tongue. Some books of etiquette for young men stressed the need for the knight to subordinate his skill at chess, if he was superior, to his desire to please his lady; ladies were told that chess would be of the greatest value in their courtship.

Murray remarks:

> At first sight, this extraordinary popularity of chess with the feudal nobility appears somewhat incredible. We unconsciously contrast the present position of chess; we lay stress on those characteristics of the game which are most prominent today, its difficulty, its seriousness, its weakness on the social side. We do not associate the mental vigour, the concentration of attention, and the powers of calculation, which are essential attributes of the chess player of the present day, with the medieval knight or feudal noble. We are at a loss to discover a reason for the general popularity of the game among a class which was distinguished by physical, rather than intellectual, prowess, and which was more at home on the battlefield or in the chase than in the hall or boudoir.

Some chess historians have advanced the explanation that nobles in the Middle Ages lived existences of paralyzing boredom, with few essential duties. Their pastimes consisted of hunting, occasional jousting, or a crusade. Thus, in the long winter nights, as the wood smoke wreathed above the vermin and the wind cut like a razor through the casement, the idle noble would turn to chess and refresh his mind. Few other games were available; it was regarded as symbolic of warfare and, contrarily, as a mime of courtly love—when the ladies took to it as well, the game's success was assured.

Pleasant though such speculations are, and no doubt with some truth, more serious explanations can be suggested.

A possibility to be explored is that chess tends to become the overriding passion in social groups that enjoy social power and position, but are excluded from the direct exercise of political power. Chess is par excellence the pastime of a disinherited ruling class that continues to crave political dominion but has seen it usurped. Just as, in psychoanalytic terms, chess is a way of sublimating Oedipal conflicts, so, in social terms, it is a device for sublimating political aspirations; the empty omnipotence exercised by the player over his pieces is consolation for lost power. It is, in general, not a preparation for regaining it.

Thus, large-scale involvement in chess among the feudal nobility appears just at the time when they are being forced to delegate power to a representative whom they do not really control—the monarch. They are losing it in two directions: to the emerging absolutist monarch and, more fundamentally, to the rising bourgeoisie. (The political formula of the centralized monarchy and enlightened despotism was, of course, to play off the bourgeoisie and the expansion of productive forces against the traditional power of the nobility and thus to wrest a margin of independent political power; this bureaucratization of feudal power was thus also a loss of power directly for the nobility, and alloyed that power with a new alien ingredient, the bourgeoisie.) Chess provided a remarkable outlet for the political frustration that this entailed. The enlarged power of the Queen—which occurred in the late fifteenth century—represented both the emergence of a stronger royal authority and the enlargement of the forces of production. Catherine de Médicis and Elizabeth I were early symbols of such trends and could not have been produced by a purely feudal social order.

The double appeal of chess probably lies in the fact that it involves not only the imaginary exercise of power, but also the imaginary attempt to destroy the monarch, thus sublimating the nobility's enormous latent hostility to the usurper.

There have been—to pursue this theme a little further—other disinherited ruling groups that nourished a chess passion:

> The Latin American oligarchy whose power was usurped both by local caudillos (from Rosas to Peron) and by the metropolitan bourgeoisie (imperialism).

> The Soviet working class, after its heroic but exhausting exertions in the October Revolution and civil war. The mass adoption of chess I describe in the next chapter as occurring after the revolution in the U.S.S.R. could not have been solely the result of bu-

reaucratic *diktat*, but must also have corresponded to deep needs felt by the proletarian masses confronted by what Brecht called "the workers' monarchy." It could be added that the dispossessed bourgeoisie there could have felt similar need, following their own canceled hopes.

The Rockingham Whigs, who enjoyed position without power and who formed the membership of the famous English chess club Parsloe's in London, in the eighteenth century.

The bourgeoisie in Germany and Austria Hungary after the defeat of the 1848 revolutions. Anderssen the Silesian schoolmaster thus logically becomes the first world chess champion.[15]

Any group engaged in a real struggle for power has no need of chess—for example, the Puritans or, in a different way, the French or British nobility after the onset of the French Revolution, which required of the nobility a real, not an imaginary, mobilization to defend position and privilege.

Some of these reflections anticipate the general narrative. To return to the Middle Ages:

From the nobility the game filtered down the social scale. From the castle the game spread to the mercenary military classes. There is some dispute as to how much it was taken up by the urban merchant orders. In many romances chess was taken as one of the attributes that distinguished the noble from the merchant, a sign of blue blood. Servants who played chess in such stories were invariably assumed to be of aristocratic origin; and the devil, in the guise of a servant, was betrayed by his skill at chess.[16] It seems likely that the game had general circulation among the middle classes in England, Spain and Italy. Chess was generally excluded from the list of forbidden pastimes in medieval town statutes, although it was sometimes specified that the stakes involved should not exceed a certain amount. Apprentices were bound by their indentures to abstain from it. The universities took a tougher line and banned chess along with dicing, jousts, hunting and hawking. Its circulation among lower orders is more dubious, though there is evidence for it. In Iceland, in the long winter nights, the game was probably played more widely than anywhere else.

Along with chess's secure status as the activity of the leisured classes there was another phenomenon—its widespread use, particularly among Church writers, as a symbol of man's condition.

The game of chess, of course, has always been regarded as a powerful image. In modern times it has been deployed as a symbol on innumerable occasions. A famous example occurs in Bergman's *Seventh Seal*, where the knight plays with death: usually in the iconography of movies, the villain is good at chess, plotting strategy over an elegant board. Normally the chess symbol remains on an extremely *kitschig* level—a kind of shorthand to indicate powers of intelligence, malign intent, elaborate plotting, et cetera.[17] Politicians are similarly fond of references to chess, normally to indicate the vastness and complexity of the strategies in which they are involved. Little of the usage of chess as symbolism tells one much about the game or its cultural meaning any more than the phrase "life's a lottery" tells one much about gambling. In general, chess as symbolism in modern times has been of small interest.

Nothing could be less true of the Middle Ages. It was characteristic of the medieval mind to detect symbolism in almost every aspect of the material world. Chess was no exception. Here is a paraphrase of one of the earliest of the medieval moralities:

> The world resembles a chess board which is chequered white and black, the colours showing the two conditions of life and death, or praise and blame. The chessmen are men of this world who have a common birth, occupy different stations and hold different titles in this life, who contend together, and finally have of common fate which levels all ranks. The King often lies under the other pieces in the bag.
>
> The King's move and power of capture are in all directions, because the King's will is law.
>
> The Queen's move is aslant only, because women are so greedy that they will take nothing except by rapine and injustice.
>
> The Rook stands for the itinerant justices who travel over the whole realm, and their move is always straight, because the judge must deal justly.
>
> The Knight's move is compounded of a straight move and an oblique one; the former betokens his legal powers of collecting rents etc., the latter his extortions and wrong-doings.
>
> The aufins [our modern bishop] are prelates wearing horns (but not like those that Moses had when he descended from Sinai). They move and take obliquely, because nearly every bishop misuses his office through cupidity.
>
> The Pawns are poor men. Their move is straight, except when they take anything; so also the poor man does well so long as he keeps from ambition. After the

Pawn is promoted he becomes a Fers and moves obliquely, which shows how hard it is for a poor man to deal rightly when he is raised above his proper station.

In this game the Devil says "Check" when a man falls into sin; and unless he quickly covers the check by turning to repentance, the Devil says "Mate" and carries him off to hell, whence there is no escape. For the devil has as many kinds of temptation to catch different types of men, as the hunter has dogs to catch different types of animals.[18]

Another morality, which apparently furnished the Estonian clergy with uplifting illustrations for nearly three hundred years, had two observations about actual chess-playing habits:

The man who postpones his repentance until death resembles a chess player who, understanding but little of the game, thinks to himself: I will allow my pieces to be taken and then at the end I will mate my opponent in the corner, while he knows all the time that his opponent is a skilful player. As there the unskilful player, so also the sinner . . . for the master-player is the Devil. . . . How can the sinner believe that he will be able to mate him in the corner—i.e., conquer at the end of his life—when the Devil tries the harder? See that you consider carefully to whom you can best give your heart from love. . . . Have you not seen how the chess player retains for a long time in his hand the piece he has lifted from the board, considering long where he will place it out of his opponent's reach? Do likewise with your heart, and take care not to place it in a shameful and dangerous place: give it rather to God.[19]

The popularity of chess from the thirteenth to the fifteenth century has never been exceeded: it was a favored pursuit of the upper classes, a common metaphor of man's condition. But from the end of the fifteenth century, it suffered, in the language of our own times, a downward mobility that was halted only at the end of the nineteenth century. According to Murray,

> the great changes in the circumstances of life, the wider activities and interests open to men of all ranks of society made games less necessary. Men no longer played games because they knew no other way of filling the hours which were without any settled occupation. They played them as a relief from other occupations, and to attract the ordinary man a game had to be less strenuous, less prolonged, less serious than chess.

There was another reason: the rise in popularity of playing cards among the leisured classes. Card games provide a far simpler means of gambling than board games, and they gradually took the place of chess as a favored occupation.

It is not really remarkable that chess should finally be ousted by a chance game as the favored activity of both upper and lower classes. Gambling, in the sense that it is always qualified by chance and propelled by cash is par excellence a game for the rich. It is an activity both of arrogance (triumph or challenge to providence) and of despair (the wild gambling excesses of a decadent aristocracy, as in eighteenth-century England or late Tsarist Russia), in which fortunes are surrendered not to force but to chance. At the other end of the scale, gambling is an activity of desperation and of masochism; it becomes the only way for a poor person to accumulate more than subsistence income; it is a prayer to providence, when no other assistance is available.

An added pressure on the popularity of chess was the increasing skill of its leading practitioners. At the start of chess in Europe there were certainly able players of old, medieval chess; but it was still at the stage of a game that has produced no chilling hierarchy of talent, where it soon becomes absurd for a tyro to try his luck with someone of more advanced skills. But with the onset of the new game (the expansion of the powers of the Queen, which I discuss below), the game started to become professionalized; its social status among the upper classes at once became more equivocal—for where "gentlemen" start encountering "players" an immediate tension in the social destiny of the game at once becomes visible. (We can follow the same sequence in tennis.)

Small wonder, therefore, that the game began to lapse in social status—not that this in itself was a bad thing, but it threw into question the social status and place of the "professional," adept in a mystery with insecure social foundations. Meanwhile, the upper classes turned to cards, and to another board game with richer possibilities —backgammon. Backgammon can admit skill; indeed, a good player will, over a series of games, always beat a bad one. Its advantage for the dilettante is that chance, however slightly, equalizes the odds and chance and the doubling dice allow a constant turnover of money.

Even at the height of chess's popularity in the Middle Ages, the players were rarely prepared to accept it as an activity divorced from gambling. There were wagers on every game, and this presented severe problems for the

Church, since many of the clerks and members of the monastic orders were extremely keen on chess. In 1062 Cardinal Damiani of Ostia wrote to the Pope asking permission to retire to a monastery, and in his letter he strongly attacks the clergy for some of their amusements. He reports that he was once on a trip with the Bishop of Florence, when the latter, instead of retiring to prayer and slumber, hurried off to the bar of the inn with the rest of the travelers. "Next morning it was told me by my groom that the aforesaid Bishop had taken the lead in chess." Damiani was outraged and denounced the Bishop. "Was it your duty at evening to take part in the vanity of chess and," says Damiani, warming to his theme, "defile your hand, the offerer of the Lord's body, and your tongue, the mediator between God and His people, by the contamination of an impious sport, especially when canonic authority decrees that Bishops who are dice players are to be deposed?" The bishop defends himself valiantly, saying that "chess is one thing, dice another," that "authority therefore forbade dice play, but by its silence permitted chess."

Damiani will have none of this, and retorts, "The decree does not mention chess, but includes the class of either game under the name *alea*.* Wherefore, when *alea* is forbidden, and nothing is said expressly of chess, it is established beyond the shadow of a doubt that each game is included under the one name, and condemned by the authority of one decision." The Bishop says he is very sorry and accepts a penance of running "carefully" through the Psalter three times and washing the feet of twelve poor men, giving them as many pieces of money

* "*Alea*," of course, is the Latin word for chance.

and food. Damiani triumphantly concludes by saying this shows "how shameful, how senseless—nay how disgusting—this sport is in a priest."

The point of the story is that both Damiani and the Bishop (finally) accepted that the game was sinful because it was often played with the help of dice. The Bishop's defense was that he had played without dice and was therefore within the law; Damiani maintained that dice were intrinsic to the game, and he persuaded the Bishop to that point of view. One can assume that what was true of the play among churchmen was true generally.

Before we trace the development of the game toward "professionalization," we should note the development of the Queen piece.

In its pre-West European guise, the piece that stood next to the King was the *Firz* (the "counselor," or "vizier"). This piece was permitted one diagonal move. Murray says that "the name Queen was a characteristically European innovation, suggested probably by the position of the piece on the board and by the general symmetry of the arrangement of the pieces, which pointed to the pairing of the two central pieces." The fact that *firz* was adopted in some of the European languages proves that the meaning of the Arab name was not understood: in Spain *alfferza*, in France *fierge*, in Middle English *fers*. In every language it had the feminine gender. In Italy, Germany and the Norse countries the piece became known as the Queen immediately. Even in English there are instances of *Queen* older than any of *Fers*.

There were some amusing complications arising from the change of gender in the piece. It was pointed out that a pawn could become a Queen, while the first Queen was still on the board. This gave rise to a scandalous social situation, bigamous and immoral.

In the 1480s two developments of great significance took place. The roles of both the Queen and the Bishop were vastly extended: the Bishop could now move freely along any diagonal, though losing the privilege of leaping over an occupied square; the Queen moving at choice to any square, diagonally, horizontally or vertically, so long as the way was clear.

The new game caught on in an astoundingly short time. Within a decade the old game had been almost completely abandoned. *Why* the Queen should suddenly have been endowed with such extended powers is a darker, though absorbing problem. There are theories that the Queen was originally introduced through a linguistic confusion between *fers*, or *fierge*, and *vierge*, meaning "maiden." Developing this notion, one writer has suggested that the introduction of the Vierge, or Queen, parallels the rise in the cult of the Virgin Mary, which took place about the same time. An even more ingenious solution is offered by Kenneth Colby, in the *Psychoanalytic Review*.

He argues (though the facts do not entirely back him up on the first point) that the development of the "wild queen's game," as it was first known, was introduced by a man rather than a woman, since men played the game more. The innovator may have felt the need for a warlike activity in which ideas are represented by pieces. By the introduction of the modern Queen, the game was made more lively from the aggressive viewpoint. The innovator, argues Colby, was probably a weakling who identified with the weak King and desired to create a strong woman who would contend against the world for him. It was postulated that he would, if he had married, have picked just such a woman to be his wife. There could have been an unconscious resemblance here to Caterina Sforza (1462–1509), who ruled Romagna ruthlessly in the stead of her husband, who was too weak to rule at all.[20]

There is something simplistic in this argument, no doubt, and it appears that there was some confusion in Colby's mind between the initial introduction of a Queen in western Europe and the development of her extended powers, which did indeed take place very suddenly, probably in northern Italy in the 1480s. Without being so precise we could say that the arrival of the "wild queen" certainly endorsed the Oedipal drama of the board. Wider conclusions about the cult of the Virgin, or indeed of the equation of the monogamous Western family with the family on the board can be and have been drawn. (We may also note that although women did play the game later—Queen Elizabeth I was a keen player—general female attendance at the board does seem to wane at about this time. By the seventeenth and eighteenth centuries the game was already becoming a male preserve.)

One could finally conjecture that the more offensive posture and abilities of the Queen (a development arising in the most economically advanced area of Europe) were a sign of the degeneration of the feudal system and the undermining of the feudal mode of warfare by more advanced technology, which transferred the advantage from defense to attack.

There is one further point on the subject of the Queen.

It has been pointed out (particularly by those keen to save chess from Freudian contamination) that Russian players cannot undergo the same Oedipal tensions as Western players, since their Queen piece still is called *Ferz* or *Krala*. The truth is more complex. The earliest authority on Russian chess shows the Queen piece being called *Korolevna* ("queen"), *Baba* ("nurse"), *Krala* ("queen"). In chess works *ferz* is now a masculine noun. But Murray tells us that in dictionaries, in the few passages in eighteenth-century works in which the word occurs, and in chess books as late as that of A. D. Petrov (1824) it is a feminine noun. The usage of *ferz* as a masculine noun appears to be due to La Bourdonnais's *Treatise on Chess*, published in Moscow in 1839. So, unless one predicates a massive revulsion by Russians against the Oedipal implications of having an overtly feminine Queen piece (which would redouble its actual significance) and a consequent renaming of the piece, it would appear that they are in somewhat the same bind as everyone else. However, even if for Russian players today the Queen piece represents a force rather than a specific gender, it does not follow that they are thereby free of Oedipal conflict. It means merely that certain aspects of the family romance are less overt.

As a footnote to this: There was an effort after the American Revolution to rename King, Queen and Pawn as "Governor," "General" and "Pioneer." This failed. Similar attempts in the Soviet Union, after the Revolution, to use terms such as "Commissar" failed also. In the Soviet Union in the twenties chess sets were made with red pieces fashioned as representatives of the proletariat and white ones as representatives of the bourgeoisie.

Over the next 350 years after the triumph of the new game, we see more and more clearly the rise of the peripatetic chess expert, wandering from country to country, settling at courts known to be friendly to the game. In fact, patronage of good players was a great feature of the sixteenth and seventeenth centuries. Throughout the last quarter of the sixteenth century and the first years of the seventeenth the great Maecenas of the chess world was Giacomo Buoncompagno, the Duke of Sora. Most of the great champions of the period played at his palace and were liberally rewarded for doing so. He gave the great Spanish player Ruy Lopez a benefice of two thousand crowns a year. Philip II of Spain was another keen patron; he once presented to Lopez a necklace of golden chain with a pendant in the form of a Rook.

The two leading Italian players of this time, Leonardo and Boi, enjoyed satisfactory patronage from the Duke of Urbino, from Pope Pius V and from King Sebastian of Portugal. Leonardo died of poison administered by a jealous rival at the palace of the Prince of Bisignano. Boi too died the victim of a poisoner; but his life had been dramatic. He had been captured by Algerian pirates and had won his freedom through his skill at chess. When he was in Naples he lived at the palace of the Duke of Urbino, who gave him a stipend of three hundred crowns a year. His extensive travels—for a time as agent for a Genovese lady—took him to Milan, to Venice, to Spain, and to Hungary, where he is reported to have played chess with Turks while riding a horse. He returned to his native Sicily in 1597, after twenty years' absence, and there traveled from town to town, playing chess. It is in-

teresting to note that in his chess-playing career Boi
made a great deal of money; his earnings, excluding
presents and the income from his appointment, amounted
to thirty thousand crowns.

Another good example of the chess professional's
career is that of Greco, who flourished in the first quarter
of the seventeenth century. He started his chess career in
Rome under the patronage of a number of wealthy prel-
ates. He left Rome to seek the fortune that was alleged to
await chess players in foreign lands. In 1621 we find him
at the court of the Duke of Lorraine, in Nancy. From
there he went to Paris and in a short time gained five
thousand crowns by his play, from such eminent players
as the Duke of Nemours. On his way to London he was
robbed of every penny he possessed. He had a successful
tour all the same in London, and after his return to Paris
he soon recouped his fortune. Next he went to Madrid,
and played well at the court of Philip IV. Finally he was
persuaded to accompany a Spanish nobleman to the West
Indies, where he died, leaving all his money to the
Jesuits.

These years, through the end of the seventeenth century, were the golden age of chess patronage. The upper
classes were still interested enough to sponsor and to pay
for excellence. In France, Catherine de Médicis was a
keen player; Henry IV played chess, and Louis XIII
(whose major addiction was hunting) had a "board" of
wool with spiked pieces to use when traveling. Henri
Jules de Bourbon had a chess academy; Queen Elizabeth
played; and although James I decried the game, Charles I
of England was an ardent player. (A letterwriter said,

"The King when he is neither in the field nor at the council passes most of his time at chess with the Marquis of Winchester.") The Puritans greatly disliked the game, presumably because it was a game, and a royal one at that. Middleton's play *A Game of Chess* had to be withdrawn in 1624, since it satirized the negotiations for Prince Charles's Spanish marriage.

With the eighteenth century came two developments: an end to the very widespread regal interest of the preceding years and the rise of the coffeehouse as a resort for players. The game still had its upper-class sponsors—the third Earl of Sunderland was a leading patron and player, and indeed wrote a Latin treatise on the game; it was to him that a French player sent an invitation for representatives of England and France to meet in a set of matches. The membership of the chess fraternity at Slaughter's Coffee House in London shows that a player could still confidently expect to survive on lordly largesse: the members included Lord Sunderland, the Earl of Godolphin, Lord Elibank, Sir Abraham Janssen, and Dr. Black, a schoolmaster from Chiswick, who obtained a royal living through his chess skill. Another member was the mathematician de Moivre, who lived for nearly thirty years on the sums he made there. Stamma, the Syrian author of a study of end games also frequented Slaughter's and was saved from bankruptcy by Lord Harrington, who kept him going.

Virtually the last example of the patronized professional was the great French player Philidor, whose chess career covered virtually the whole of the last half of the eighteenth century. He was famous also as a musician. His first motet was performed at Versailles when he was only eleven; in a curious way he presages the prodigies who became such a feature of chess life later on.

Philidor took up chess as a career when a musical engagement he had undertaken in Holland collapsed in 1745. He was stranded in Rotterdam, but found enough British officers in residence (since the English army was in Holland) to pay him for his games and introduce him to gentlemen. He traveled to London and enjoyed a great success at Slaughter's. Returning to Holland, he looked to friends among the British officers for subscriptions to his book on chess. Lord Sandwich subscribed for ten copies and the Duke of Cumberland for fifty.[21]

Philidor, after the success of his book, went to Berlin in 1750, since he had heard that Frederick the Great was a keen player. They did not play, though Philidor gave some blindfold exhibition games. He returned to Paris, where the Café de la Régence had become the focal center of French chess life. When he returned to London in 1772 a chess club called Parsloe's was formed, with a three-guinea subscription and membership limited to one hundred. It started as one of the most fashionable clubs in London. In 1776 the members included Charles James Fox, the Marquis of Rockingham, Lord Mansfield, Erskine, Gibbon, and General Burgoyne. Murray remarks that

> it was the last rally of the English nobility to claim chess as the game most typical of their order, and it was part of the irony of fate that the man for whose benefit the club was established should have done most by his literary labours to destroy this historic connection with chess. For it was the diffusion of analysis and the rise in the standard of play which re-

sulted in the realization of the principles of the game, which effected the change. The chess player now had to study if he wished to excel.

The age of the amateur was over—so far as top-level play was concerned.

Just how fickle the class support of the game was can be shown by the fact that this brilliant patronage vanished within thirteen years. In France, Monsieur le Comte de Provence, later Louis XVIII, had been the patron of the chess club near the Palais Royal. A comparison of the membership lists of the two clubs between 1777 and 1790 shows that even in England (as, not surprisingly, in Paris) the upper classes had moved away en bloc. Only fourteen members attended the opening dinner at Parsloe's to launch the season in 1790. It became the resort of chess players only.

By the 1830s the chess world as we know it today was beginning to form: The first chess column which ran regularly for a while started in the Liverpool *Mercury*. It lasted a year. The longest-surviving column was started by Staunton in the *Illustrated London News* in 1842. The earliest chess magazine was the *Palamède*, launched in 1836, but soon discontinued. The longest-surviving English magazine, the *British Chess Magazine*, was started in 1881. The German *Schachzeitung* started in 1846.

The first International Tournament was held in London in 1851. It was organized by Staunton and won by Anderssen, the schoolmaster from Breslau, who could thus fairly regard himself as the first World Champion. But Anderssen supported himself by schoolmastering and not by chess. Indeed, Morphy used some of the prize money from his great victories in Paris to defray Anderssen's expenses for the journey from Germany. Players were now uncertain as to their social role, as the game became a mode of relaxation for the bourgeoisie and the pursuit of players who were practically professionals. Morphy, as we know, was morbidly sensitive—as a "gentleman"—on the subject of financial rewards for his performance. Staunton consistently emphasized that his "serious" life was the one devoted to Shakespearean scholarship.

The game was no longer generously patronized by the aristocracy, and thus the professional chess player was confronted with very serious problems in the matter of supporting himself. Although he found it possible to earn enough money to feed himself through playing chess in the Viennese cafés, Steinitz finally died alone, mad and bankrupt. Throughout a long career he had never been able to save enough money to relinquish the rigors of continuous tournament play. Lasker never was prosperous; Capablanca survived through the patronage of the Cuban government. One could attribute many of the darker phases of Alekhine's career, such as his promulgation of Nazi doctrine, to the need to gain some form of patronage. Euwe supported himself through teaching, and from the end of World War II until 1972 the championship remained in Russia, where players enjoyed the support of the state. As we shall see in the discussion of Fischer, a large amount of the alarums before the match in Iceland concerned the generation of sufficient cash to match Fischer's estimation of his profession. To garner the appropriate sum, chess had to be converted into a modern spectacle with the whole at-

tendant apparatus of television rights, predicted publishers' advances, and the rest. There were added la-
gniappes such as the promise of financial support from
Jim Slater, the London financier. (There is a paradoxical
truth that Fischer failed to realize the maximum profit
potential of his triumph—as the disappointed moans of
New York publishers and others throughout 1973 bore
witness. See the chapter on Fischer.)

In this professionalization of chess much of the color
and drama of the game's transactions in the early days
disappeared. It became, as Reider says, "a mathematical
science with a somewhat masculine, homosexual flavour." The overt projection of the game's tensions, which
resulted in fist fights between husband and wife in the
twelfth century, became repressed into an austere etiquette, where the cry "*j'adoube*" accompanied each adjustment of a piece. More and more the game became
work. As C. H. O'D. Alexander remarks in his little book
on the Fischer-Spassky match:

> Social chess is played for fun; competitive chess is
> work and very hard work indeed—and while it can
> give very deep satisfaction, it is the kind of satisfac-
> tion and fulfilment one gets from work not play. In
> a chess tournament you will often see masters playing
> quick offhand games (at the rate of five or ten min-
> utes per game) for relaxation; this is chess for fun—
> and in these games the players are recovering the
> kind of pleasure one gets when one first discovers one's
> talent and before the game has become work.[22]

In fact, Alexander makes money in one of the few
ways a chess player can: he writes about it. It is one of
the fondest hopes of a professional or top-level chess

player to have a chess column in a newspaper, which will thus allow him the essential coincidence between "work" and earning money.

But it is a mysterious kind of work, and one that is conducted in odd settings. In the eighteenth century, for example, chess had a very self-assured social and intellectual setting, in the Café de la Régence in Paris. As Diderot remarks at the start of *Rameau's Nephew*, "If the weather is too cold or rainy, I take shelter in the Régence café, where I entertain myself by watching chess being played. Paris is the world center, and this café is the Paris center for the finest skill at this game." Robespierre would play there; and later still Napoleon. The great Morphy games took place there too.[23]

This is the kind of locale for chess that Fischer would presumably have endorsed. In an interview in the early 1960s he pronounced himself eager to open a chess club on the socially acceptable Upper East Side of Manhattan —with only smartly dressed folk admitted; no bums. His wish reflects the increasing *déclassment* of the game to seedier and seedier locales, such as the Chess & Checker Club on 42nd Street, in Manhattan. In some ways there is a parallel here with billiards, once also an upper-class game, but now played to perfection in the pool halls portrayed in Robert Rossen's marvelous film *The Hustler*.[24] Fischer's dream of a tasteful club on the Upper East Side is an anachronism—the Palace of Philip II or Parsloe's, rather than the Chess & Checker Club. The latter is the reality. The other reality is the tournament circuit: rundown seaside towns in England, such as Bournemouth or Hastings; or Curaçao; or even—ironically, in view of Zweig's suicide there—Petrópolis.

Work that is not work in the socially recognized form of that activity must lead to psychological pressures on the "worker." A sport or activity where absolute expertise has no convenient slot in society (in so far as financial reward or public recognition are concerned) can produce *angst* and neurosis. (A great many Westerns and Japanese samurai movies deal with the destiny of a hero equipped with a skill that has become both socially useless and socially unacceptable.) It is not, therefore, merely because of Oedipal tension and regression—the breakdown of the sublimating powers of the game—that many chess players in the late-nineteenth and twentieth centuries have exhibited signs of derangement. Their lives are determined by the actual nature of the game; by the interpersonal tensions generated by it; by the situation of chess as an intense but fringe "play-work" activity, played on the margins of society for little money and limited *réclame*. The more the expertise the greater the repression. The sexual sublimation is paralleled by the social dislocation. A sad destiny.

CHAPTER SIX

Proletarian, Socialist Chess

Chess, as we have seen, has never lacked advocates to commend its virtues as mind trainer, logic teacher, fashioner of will and character. But only in the Soviet Union has it been actively encouraged as a pursuit by the state. Over the past 40-odd years we have seen the fruits of that encouragement, in the procession of Soviet champions in the chess arena, terminated only in 1972 by Fischer. Seldom has a game received such stimulation from official circles or so much direct political benediction.[1]

Chess had enjoyed a substantial career in Russia, even before the Revolution. Travelers had noted the prevalence of the game, not only among the more prosperous classes but among the masses as well. A writer in the *Critical Review* for 1792 remarked, "In a free government the Russian might appear with equal advantage as in the military department; intelligent, active, reflecting, and endowed with a spirit of calculation. He might succeed in every pursuit; at present he excels only in chess."

Lord Taylor, writing in the London *Sunday Times* in 1962 ruminated on the affinity of the Russians for chess:

133

Pure paranoia is a rare mental illness whose synonym is systematized delusional insanity. Its essence is that it combines suspicion with organized tortuosity. All of us are apt to become paranoid at times, to think others are talking about us or even scheming against us. Almost always we are wrong. In business and litigation, politics and war, a small measure of paranoia may be a useful protective mechanism. But, as a rule, paranoid feelings are a disadvantage to both parties in the situation. *There is only one place where, as a temporary expedient, a paranoid approach is a positive advantage—on the chessboard.* It will be obvious at once that the Russians have more than their fair share of paranoia. It is a national handicap, which they are only starting to overcome.

Actually, had Lord Taylor been brooding on the Russian character in the nineteenth rather than the twentieth century, he would also have had to deal with gambling, which certainly plays a more substantial role in nineteenth-century fiction, notably in the works of Dostoevsky, who hated chess, and was enough of a gambling addict to experience—as he reported it—an orgasm at a moment of particularly heavy loss.

But despite the shameful record of Dostoevsky, chess had an attractive pedigree when it came under consideration by Bolshevik leaders as a mass activity. Marx played it and became extremely ill-tempered when he lost. Tolstoy and Turgenev played it. Lenin played it, and even said that it taught strategy and tactics. He was a good loser; interested, so Gorki said, more in the nature of the combination that had beaten him than in the fact that he lost. He gave it up when he found it interfering with political activity. Clearly, Russia had also produced top chess players. Tchigorin was among the best players in the world, and as we have seen, Alekhine was already coming into prominence at the time of the First World War.

The first really significant figure in the Soviet chess world was A. F. Ilyin-Zhenevsky (1894-1941). He had joined the Bolsheviks at school, and after 1917 he held important posts in the government and the Party. Early in 1920 he was appointed Chief Commissar at the headquarters of the General Reservists Organization, known as Vsevobuch. This body was set up after the Revolution to provide elementary physical and military training for people before their conscription into the Red Guards and later the Red Army. Under the aegis of Vsevobuch military sports clubs were set up in factories and railway centers.

Ilyin-Zhenevsky hit on the idea of including chess in preconscription training programs.

> I was prompted to put forward this proposal by noticing that when sport came under discussion, it was valued not so much from the standpoint of its effects on physical well-being, as from the standpoint of its influence on the character. The chief value of sport, it was claimed, is that it develops in a man mental qualities which are of supreme importance in a soldier. Here a parallel with chess involuntarily suggested itself. After all, chess too, and in some ways even more than sport, develops in a man boldness, presence of mind, composure, a strong will and, most important, a sense of strategy. My proposal was accepted . . . Soon in our Vsevobuch magazine, *K Novoi Armii*, I opened the first chess column.

By 1920 there were two schools of thought. One wished to resurrect the prewar Russian chess federation; the other hoped to make chess part of the new revolutionary culture. Ilyin-Zhenevsky was uncompromising on this point. Chess must become integral to the new socialist culture. It should have a right to exist only if it was popularized among the masses. "In this country, where the workers have gained the victory, chess cannot be apolitical, as in capitalist countries." The task of chess was seen as extensive. As phrased by A. Kogan, a Soviet chess historian, "From the point of view of the revolutionary vanguard of the proletariat chess is not an end in itself but a means of raising the cultural (and thereby also the political) level of the laboring masses in the world."

A brisk political battle followed these pronouncements. In January of 1924 the Ministry of Internal Affairs approved the constitution of the apolitical chess federation, based in Petrograd. The decision was reversed in August of that year: the huge chess section organized by the Moscow Trades Union Council refused to join the federation. The nonunion Moscow clubs supported the council, and the apolitical loungers of Petrograd were routed.

The third All-Union Congress was held in late 1924. Further staunch statements about chess followed. The organizing committee saw chess as

> a powerful weapon of intellectual culture, a weapon in the struggle for a higher cultural level. Chess is not a game, or more accurately far from merely a game. Chess stimulates, develops and disciplines thought. There is no other game in which pure logic and logical

deduction approach so close to the abstract forms of mathematical thinking. This fact alone gives chess enormous educational importance. But that is not all. At the same time chess is a struggle that demands a great effort of will. In this way it disciplines not only thought in general but also the will. The infinite number of combinations that unfold at all stages of a game of chess develop in a player firstly the ability to orientate himself, then great caution, which every even slightly experienced player learns, and finally accuracy of calculation. All this together develops in the player persistence, insight and caution and the ability quickly to orientate himself in various circumstances. These qualities taken together show all the attributes of an intellectually and psychologically perfect type of individual.

As if this were not enough, the committee added that it

regards chess as a political weapon that must be used in order (a) to give to the working masses, tired after their daily labor, a rational leisure activity, and (b) to exploit the educational significance of chess . . . in order with its help to give a new impetus to the growth of the intellectual culture and the training of the mind among the laboring masses.

This Congress approved the inauguration of a new body to superintend Soviet chess; an All-Union chess section was created, attached to the Supreme Council for Physical Culture of the Russian S.F.S.R. Its chairman was N. V. Krylenko. The importance attached to chess can be seen from Krylenko's career. In 1918 he had been briefly Commissar of War, following a spell as Comman-

der in Chief of Russian forces. In 1918 he was Public
Prosecutor for the Revolutionary Tribunals; in 1931 he
was Commissar of Justice of the R.F.S.R.; in 1936 he was
Commissar of Justice of the U.S.S.R.; and in 1938 he was
shot.

In 1926 the Leningrad section opened a course for
chess instructors. The number of registered chess players
rose from 1,000 in 1923, to 24,000 in 1924, to 140,000 in
1928.

In 1925 an international tournament was held in Moscow. The Russian Bogolyubov triumphed over Capablanca, Marshall, Tartakover, Torre, Reti and other contemporary grand masters. This was before Bogolyubov
became a figure for denunciation, along with Alekhine.
Earlier in the year the chess leadership had pondered
the question of competition with bourgeois players. Since
it would obviously be a coup if local players were to win,
the statement showed common sense:

> The chess section considers that in certain condi-
> tions the participation of working-class chess players
> in bourgeois tournaments would be politically advan-
> tageous, inasmuch as it would unite the workers
> round the idea of class solidarity and of their opposi-
> tion as a class to the bourgeoisie. From this standpoint
> the chess section admits the possibility of the prole-
> tarian chess organization's participation in interna-
> tional tournaments, in order through victories over
> bourgeois masters to increase among the proletarian
> masses self-respect and faith in their youthful talents.

At this tournament three Soviet psychologists were
unleashed on the masters, to test them on their powers of

memory, attention, intellect, imagination and character.[2] The report was not without interest.

They found that outside chess matters the masters' memory was not exceptional, attention was characterized less by intensity than by the ability to range widely and grasp dynamic relationships. They showed high powers of logical reasoning but did not work quickly. The Soviet psychologists divided them into two groups: the poets and the pedants—but added that their thought processes were both abstract and highly concrete; and that they showed no sign of emotional instability.

They also worked out a chess psychogram, enumerating the sixteen physical and psychological qualities required to do well at chess. These included strength and general health; nerves; self-control; distribution of attention over many areas; perception of dynamic roles; contemplative turn of mind; high intellectual development; ability to think concretely; ability to think objectively; powerful memory for chess matters; powers of synthetical thought and imagination; disciplined emotions; self-confidence.

Even with this splendid list, the psychologists were not finished, and they finally paid their dues with the following deformation of Marxism:

> What word can convey all the essential features of chess, indicating both its complexity and its unity? The only word that can satisfy these demands is *dialectics*.
>
> The general pattern of the dialectical process is revealed in the external arrangement of the game. The alternating moves of the two opponents are the expression of two mutually opposing sets of interests

and plans, interests and strivings. In this way the basis of the dialectical process—movement based on contradiction, transition from assertion to denial—is preserved in chess in its full force . . . each new position in the game is conditioned equally by the development of one player's plan and by the moves of his opponent. The objective unfolding of the game as a whole is a result of a synthesis of two ideas and intentions.

This kind of thing is strongly reminiscent of the medieval explications quoted in the last chapter. Curiously, the Soviet psychologists did hint that there was something a little more complex about games and chess than the mere creation of the perfect man. They allowed that games satisfied "demands and strivings that lie deep in man's nature, but fail to find satisfaction in everyday life . . . they provide release from psychophysical tensions caused by everyday routine . . . as an activity motivated from within, games are satisfying in themselves, pure experience stripped of any utilitarian significance."

This last sentence was, of course, in direct contradiction to the general tenor of Soviet notions about chess, since it was precisely the utilitarian significance that they were interested in.

In 1924, when the Fédération Internationale des Echecs (FIDE) was set up, the Russians refused to join it. At that time the official attitude was that chess contributed toward working-class international unity, that "a working-class player of the Argentine can easily correspond with a German worker in the language of their art—that is, via the chessboard." Accordingly, they declared that "Russian chess organizations not only were not politically neutral, but indeed stood quite firmly on the platform of class warfare and the international working-class movement; consequently it was quite impossible for them to enter an international organization which did not share this platform."

Instead they joined, indeed sponsored, the Workers Chess International, founded in Hamburg three years earlier. At the height of its activity the members outside the U.S.S.R. numbered twenty thousand and held an international tournament (in which the Comintern presumably took great interest) in 1927. This body was riven by political dispute between the Communists and the Socialists. The Communists wanted it to be an active revolutionary organization devoted to violent class warfare and the Socialists did not. By 1929 life became impossible. The Soviet section resigned from the organization and set up a chess section attached to the Socialist Workers Sports International.

Chess reached the summit of its career as a utilitarian weapon in the battle to boost production in 1928. This was the year of the announcement of the first Five-Year Plan. Kogan, in his history, reports that "one must record the decisive turn taken in 1929 toward saturating all chess work with a Communist content and linking it with tasks of socialist construction."

There was a torrent of pronouncements from on high about the duties of chess players in respect to the Plan— "The present widespread interest in chess and chess tournaments must be transformed into competitions to raise productivity. . . . In time the situation must be reached wherein every chess-playing worker in the U.S.S.R.

must be a leader of socialist competition in industry."
Chess players were regarded as an elite group—

> A chess player must possess certain mental qualities
> which number him among the most conscious work-
> ers, consequently the chess organization has every
> right to demand that chess workers should be in the
> front ranks of the building of socialism, of technical
> mastery and of the rapid and successful fulfillment
> of the First Five Year Plan for the socialist construc-
> tion of the Soviet economy.

In the midst of these urgings for every chess player to
be a Stakhanovite leader, we can detect some murmur-
ings of unease—as though it was dawning on some com-
rades in the chess secretariat that chess players tend to be
interested in doing nothing much else than playing
chess, and that the game does not necessarily increase
productivity. There are hints at this time that chess in
the trade-unions is felt to be not political enough; people,
families even, were merely consorting in central trade-
union clubrooms or libraries and chatting with workers
from other factories. Even the class composition of these
groups was arousing unease. Reviewing the situation, a
chess commissar remarked that

> such a mixed group of intellectuals, united by noth-
> ing but chess, naturally led to a situation where the
> club concentrated on competitions and champion-
> ships, while the industrial and political tasks facing
> chess players received no attention. Consequently po-
> litical disinterestedness flourished, under cover of
> which chess circles harbored sentiments remote from,
> or even hostile to, the proletariat.

This was ominous, and Krylenko followed through by attacking those who were complaining about his constant emphasis on the politicization of chess. This did not save him from being purged in 1938, "for cutting chess off from the sociopolitical life of the nation."

Some cynicism about the uplifting effects of chess—but also evidence about its sudden prominence in Soviet culture—is provided in Ilf and Petrov's splendid satire *Twelve Chairs* (1926). The confidence trickster Osip Bender appears in the town of Vashuki and announces that he will give an exhibition of simultaneous chess. He lectures the inhabitants of the seedy little town on its virtues: " 'Chess, a game that spells progress in culture. Chess increases the prosperity of the country. If you approve my idea [to finance his games] you will be walking down marble steps from the town to the quay! Vashuki will become the capital of ten countries.' Dazzling visions of the future appeared before the eyes of the Vashukian chess lovers. The very room they were in seemed to have grown into a vast hall. The moldy walls of the racing stables receded and disappeared and were replaced by a thirty-story chess castle in the air, throughout which, in every marbled recess, even in the high-speed elevators as they flashed up and down, people were playing on chessboards inlaid with malachite. Marble steps led down to the blue waters of the Volga. Ocean-going vessels are anchored in the river. A long line of cars moves between rows of marble hotels. In a sudden hush the champion José Raul Capablanca is seen going for a stroll. He is surrounded by exotic foreign ladies. A policeman salutes; he is dressed in a special checkered uniform embroidered with golden knights . . ." Even-

tually Bender is exposed as a fraud: but not before the
people of Vashuki have proved themselves most receptive
to his visions.

Despite Krylenko's strictures, and satirical assault, Soviet chess was firmly established by the middle thirties.
The first great triumph, in purely nationalist terms,
came with Botvinnik's victory in the Nottingham tournament of 1936. It was regarded as the vindication of
the whole Soviet chess program. *Pravda* hailed the event
with huge articles, which are still quoted today in the
U.S.S.R. as expressions of the official attitude to the
game—

> We value this wise game, standing on the frontier be-
> tween art and science . . . Our great teachers Marx
> and Lenin devoted themselves enthusiastically to
> chess in their leisure hours. . . . Nowadays in the
> most distant corners of our land there are chess clubs,
> in remote villages, collective farms, from the moun-
> tain settlements of Dagestan to the villages of central
> Asia there are chess clubs. . . . Recently an All-
> Union Chess and draughts Congress of pig-breeders,
> dairymen and zoo technicians met in the Stalin state
> farm, situated in the Moscow region twelve miles
> from the nearest railway station. An endless number
> of such instances could be brought forward . . . The
> U.S.S.R. is becoming the classical land of chess. . . .
> The unity of feelings and will of the whole country,
> the careful attention and care paid to people by the
> Soviet government, the Communist Party, and, above
> all, by Comrade Stalin—these are the sources of So-
> viet victories. . . .

The article concluded with this astonishing rhapsody:

Sitting at the chess table in Nottingham, Botvinnik could not fail to sense that the whole country was watching every move of the wooden pieces on his board and that the whole country, from the most remote corners to the Kremlin towers, was wishing him success and giving him moral support. He could not fail to sense the powerful breathing of his great motherland. That is why he played so calmly and confidently, that is why he could allow himself the luxury of playing aggressively, moving away from old, stereotyped patterns of play.

Botvinnik (the Ministry of Heavy Industry announced), "for successfully combining his technical studies with achievements in chess is awarded an automobile." As Richards remarks in *Soviet Chess*, "It is understandable that so much should be made of Botvinnik's achievement; at last the aim of catching up with the West, set before the whole of Soviet society, had been realized in one field."

Botvinnik's victory also impelled writers to discern a style of Soviet chess. Krylenko stressed that "we see two styles, two types of play, characteristic of Soviet art and the art of the dying bourgeois world." Another writer, Spokoiny said in 1936, "The Soviet style of chess, as is generally recognized, is characterized by its aggressiveness. . . . Surely, the main characteristic of the Soviet style is the element of struggle. The Soviet style is the Stakhanovite movement—struggle and victory! 'Stalin demands victories!' said the poet, Lakhuti. And the Stakhanovites struggle and are victorious."

There is nothing quite so eventful in the years that followed. Botvinnik became world champion in 1946, and as we know, the Russians maintained their grip on the championship until 1972. In 1964 the Soviet Chess Federation remarked that there were 3½ million members and that this should rise. By the 1960s, even though it had been true before, Soviet masters were quite frank about their vocation. "We are professionals of course," said Tal, "competing in tournaments, working on chess theory, visiting small towns for simultaneous displays."

By the 1960s, amid the excesses of Khrushchevite revisionism there were some warning noises about the political laxity of chess players. The Soviet chess magazine stated that "our daily task is to educate chess players toward communist consciousness, love of labor and discipline and loyalty to the good of society." But it was revealed the Soviet chess players were falling short of the required standards. Local chess authorities, instead of reforming the miscreants, were turning a blind eye to their activities. A 1964 article reported that "Master Nikolaevsky has been disqualified for bad behavior. For a long time Master Yukhtman has done no socially useful work. Two Moscow players, Master Zakharov and candidate Master Dubinsky, have neglected their studies. There are cases of immorality and of weakness for alcohol. Certain leading players have avoided visiting local clubs and competing in 'uninteresting tournaments.' . . ."

Various considerations arise from this remarkable history. Firstly, the social function of games, as seen by the Bolshevik leaders: a pursuit in which the masses were to be encouraged should aid production. They were confronted with a proletariat whose leisure was frequently spent in drink and gambling. Chess was an answer. As one writer put it, "In our country, where the cultural level is comparatively low, where up till now a typical pastime of the masses has been brewing liquor, drunkenness and brawling, chess is a powerful means of raising the general cultural level."

Secondly, they regarded chess as a powerful weapon in the struggle against superstition. In 1928 Lunacharsky, Commissar for Education, had made an attack on card playing: "The player is dependent on chance phenomena and every card player has a belief in fate and luck. Hence, no people are more superstitious than card players. In this sense it is a corrupting pastime that reproduces the disorganized life of bourgeois society, where there is a perpetual struggle between people and where man is dependent on fate." He went on to praise chess. Similar views were expressed by Rokhlin, a historian of Russian chess: "Chess thought is based on independent creative analysis, justified by its practical consequences; in chess there is no element of chance, no depending on providence; chess by its nature is international. All these facts make it a true weapon and a living piece of propaganda against religious delusions." (It would be interesting to know what he would have made of Fischer's religious proclivities.)

There were other advantages—among them, that it was cheap. No costly sports facilities or swimming pools; merely a room and some boards.

Nor is it surprising that there were such efforts to proletarianize chess. Quite apart from the ideological and political necessities, writers such as Ilyin-Zhenevsky were well aware of the social status of chess in western Europe; his statement on the social destiny of chess in the U.S.S.R. has a noble, though ironic, ring to it:

> Our task is not the training of chess players, competing for high-sounding titles and money prizes, in pursuit of world renown, remote from life and enclosed in a narrow caste, infinitely remote from society; not competition for the sake of competition in an atmosphere of openly expressed gambling under the corrupt influence of the western-European bourgeois café. . . . What class does chess serve in capitalist countries? To answer this question, it is enough to remember that the centers of chess life in most bourgeois countries are first-class cafés. In Paris there was for a long time the Café de la Régence, in Berlin the café König, in Vienna the café Rabel, in Riga the Reuter café, in Geneva the Café de la Couronne. Almost exclusively wealthy people gather in these cafés. A working man, if he were poorly dressed, would simply not be let in. And furthermore, every visit to this sort of café is rather expensive. . . .

Where the error came was not so much in the desire to proletarianize chess—though, as we have seen in connection with the first Five Year Plan, it had an instrumental purpose—but in the conclusion that talent in chess could be equated with talent in any other activity. There is no evidence for this assumption, even if it might be true, as Rokhlin reported, that old men in the factories who took up chess, became literate to read about chess and therefore became generally literate.

Furthermore, the chess commissars never seemed to have asked themselves, and their psychologists, apart from Herbstman, never suggested, that the emotions activated in chess might be profoundly nonsocialist, in the sense that the player certainly is motivated by an individual, aggressive desire to win (and in this point we need not bring in psychoanalytic implications, even more damaging, as to *why* he has this aggressive desire to win).

One great advantage of the game, though it may not have occurred to the policy makers initially, is that it is nonpolitical—in fact it is profoundly quietist. Chess, after all, is played at remote control, in correspondence chess, or one to one. It is silent. It is nonfigurative, in the sense that it is conducted purely in its own terms, not in generally current concepts or political or cultural ideas. Therefore, entirely unlike the early efforts in the artistic sphere proper, there was no possibility of bringing people collectively together in the expression of revolutionary ideas which might be subversive or discommoding to the political leadership. All that chess players could do, after all, was play their game and get on with the tasks of raising production—which would be the ideal of any state, keen on endorsing some safe leisure activity.

There is something ironic, in this context, in the fact that the Soviet Union endorsed an art-for-art's sake activity from the early twenties onward with chess. It was an activity whose only justification was itself. There was indeed no evidence that it did help to boost production, and one can opine that it may have done the opposite. Real art for art's sake, in the bourgeois world, was in the event very political, in the sense that it was an affront to middle-class morals and standards. But rather like the English detective story and the crossword puzzle, chess was a perfect leisure activity: politically safe, sedate, and noncollective.

One must beware, all the same, of imputing excessive powers of manipulation and *dirigisme* to the party or to the state. To restate a suggestion of the last chapter, the mass adoption of chess after the revolution could never have been solely the result of bureaucratic *diktat*. It must have corresponded to a need of the proletarian masses, confronted by the rise of the "Workers Monarchy," and exhausted after the triumphs of the Revolution and the ordeals of the civil war. And again, one must make a distinction between chess as the passion of an isolated individual, and the mass pastime of a group "exiled" from political power.

Botvinnik presents a startling comparison to his predecessor, Alekhine, as world champion. Alekhine died alone and wretched in Portugal, the victim of much political abuse for his probable cooperation with the Nazis. Botvinnik is an honored citizen of the Soviet Union, has enjoyed a chess career almost as prolonged as Lasker's. Not much evidence is available on his character; but he is married and is a successful engineer. His manner of play was aggressive, and Botvinnik himself has written that his kind of game was dynamically capable of meeting any situation that might arise, as opposed to the more static conceptions of capitalist chess.

Botvinnik represented the spearhead of the new Soviet champions. His confident and strong personality does seem to suggest that official support, consciousness of representing his country in an area where it could match and overtake the West, conspired to reduce the psychic tension and disfigurements that characterized some of his Western colleagues. In his person is represented the success of Ilyin-Zhenevsky's vision.

It is clear that recent years have seen a falling-away from the great years of Soviet socialist chess achievements. Even though Russians held the championship until 1972, the younger players do not seem to have been of quite the same disciplined outlook as Botvinnik. There seems to have been increasing tension between the views of the official bureaucracy of chess and those of the players, who favored a more professional, less political viewpoint—"Obviously many people forget," said Petrosian (world champion between 1963 and 1969), "that nowadays in chess the struggle for points prevails over creative considerations. . . . It is naïve to think that it is expedient (let alone possible) for a player striving for the top place in a tournament to play every game all out, putting all his creative energy into one encounter."

The equivocal figure of Boris Spassky somewhat confirms dubiety about the present course of Soviet chess. He was born in Leningrad in 1937. He lived through the siege of Leningrad: he was the second child and eldest son of the family and in 1944 his father was divorced from his mother. "From six or seven I was the chief in my family," he remarked to one biographer. Spassky learned to play chess at the age of five and started to play seriously just after World War II. At the age of eighteen he had won the World Junior Championship. But during the late fifties his chess career was compromised by uncertainty in play and some censure for failing to have trained properly. He was getting on badly with his first wife, whom he divorced in 1961; and his trainer, Alexander Tolush, was not satisfactory for him. Apparently

Tolush had a sharp temper and a biting tongue, and possibly he was jealous of Spassky. In 1961 Spassky changed trainers to Bondarevsky, "sympathetic in temperament and without personal ambitions."[3] In 1966 he remarried. In 1969 he took the world championship from Petrosian.

Spassky is the classic "nice guy," in sporting iconography. In Iceland he was constantly contrasted to Fischer. He displayed perfect manners, and comported himself with restraint, except for one moment when he confided to a writer that he would like to kick Fischer in the behind. There is, of course, another side to this elegant demeanor. No one becomes world champion of chess without having a ferocious desire to win. He displays enthusiasm for the writings of Dostoevsky, which is not usually a passion for anyone with a perfectly balanced psyche. One could surmise the following, on the most provisional and simplistic level: that Spassky suffered guilt, after the departure of his father—which represented the triumph of his Oedipal fantasies but also remorse for the "murder" of his father: that in the familiar pattern these repressed anxieties were sublimated in the ritual "father murder/defense of father" of chess.[4] (Dostoevsky, incidentally, believed that he had killed his father.) However, this sublimation was complicated by the imposition of a severe trainer—Tolush—who, in the fatherlike persona of the trainer exacerbated the tension which the game should have been sublimating. The arrival of a gentler, more maternal trainer seems to have led to an immediate improvement in his play. The very intensity of his "good manners," carried almost to excess in Iceland, seems to indicate the depths of the repression of his sadistic urges, suddenly revealed by his statement about Fischer, "I would like to kick him up the bottom!" as he aimed a vicious kick in the air. However the repressed guilt still breaks through the sublimation, causing the lapses in his play for which he is noted.

The full paranoia of the suggestion that Fischer's chair in Iceland had a deadly ray in it, incapacitating to Spassky is a further indication of Russian prostration before the madness induced by chess.

Added to these personal tensions are the social tensions of modern chess life in the Soviet Union. Great things are still expected of the Soviet Grand Master. He is expected to represent his people, comport himself with dignity, and win. Spassky himself has exhibited sympathy for the Czech grandmaster Ludek Pachman, imprisoned in 1968 for his role in resistance to the Soviet invasion. Beyond such scanty evidence of a qualified attitude to the policies of his nation, he has expressed impatience with the chess authorities. Most crucially of all, he said in 1970 that "Chess is a very hard profession. . . . *Our labor should be respected more than it is*" (my italics). These words from the world champion, in the only country that endorses chess as a profession at all, in terms of official rewards, soft option jobs and material conveniences!

Such a remark strikingly recalls the despairing assessments of their social predicament uttered by Western players. The wheel has come full circle. The Soviet Union created and fostered their professional chess players, as a deliberate contrast to procedures in the West. The author of the *Soviet School of Chess* wrote that "in the hands of the imperialist bourgeoisie physical education, including sport, is the means of preparing cannon fodder for aggressive wars, a means of increasing the exploitation of the workers and of dulling their consciousness. Bourgeois sport inflames low passions and cripples men spiritually and physically. It is ruled by the laws of private enterprise and the profit motive." Now these are noble sentiments, and it was a splendid vision, of such people as Ilyin-Zhenevsky and others in the twenties—a vision that strove to promote recreational activities which represented the obverse of this dark picture.

There was a period when the policy of fostering the "mass line" in chess did work. At a time of much adversity for the Soviet Union, Botvinnik scored brilliant triumphs all over the world, and seemed an advertisement for the achievements of Soviet culture. No doubt it was preferable that some portion of the masses should refresh itself with chess rather than playing cards and vodka. But what an irony for a socialist society to have achieved its greatest cultural triumphs in the arena of chess—a parody of what the emancipation of the human personality can involve. And so the Soviet chess professionals find themselves involved in an activity that is lauded by party and state, that is not fun but *work*. They know it is *work*, but work is justified in the eyes of the authorities only by *victory*. The players' vision of the meaning of victory may be becoming as qualified as that of the athletes who have refused to honor their national anthems on the Olympic podium. For the players, victory may mean a purely personal triumph in their lonely activity, an activity not really understood by their sponsors. In conditions of scarcity and absence of material comforts, and in the full rush of national or revolutionary fervor such egotism may be surmounted. But over half a century after the Revolution this may become less simple. For Spassky and his younger colleagues, the future may hold less respect for chess, less social sanction; and the game may gradually move toward the margins of society and social approval.

There is something bizarre about the whole Soviet chess experience—from the battles fought in the Red Chess International, to the importance of chess to the first Five Year Plan, to the reaction to Botvinnik's triumphs, to Spassky's shamefaced return to Moscow in 1972— something tragic too, in that a revolutionary culture should have found a receptacle smelling so strongly of neurosis, loneliness, sterility.

A FOOTNOTE ON CHESS, DIPLOMACY AND WAR

"We play poker, they play chess" used to be the adage at one school for international relations in the United States. It was also, it seems, a favored phrase of President Kennedy. The thought behind the words was that the Communist enemy, in all his Oriental cunning, had a strategy thoroughly conceived and inherently rational: move would be countered by move; and uncertainty and chance eliminated. "We," on the other hand, play poker. "We" gamble and bluff.

As we have seen, the emphasis on the enemy's playing chess has a venerable ancestry in high and low art. But where the little maxim about chess and poker goes seriously wrong is in the supposition that "our side" is not interested in conceiving of war or diplomacy in chess terms. In ancient and in modern times the very opposite has been the case. We have seen that legend has chess being invented as a rehearsal or exemplar of war. There are innumerable examples of generals and statesmen expressing enthusiasm for chess, and their suggestion that their own trade is simply conducted on a larger board. In the popular imagination, mirroring such sentiments, international affairs are often conceived in terms of chess imagery. Hardly an issue of *Punch* magazine in the nineteenth century was complete without a cartoon of "the chessboard of Europe" simulating the play of policy and maneuver.

The July 1972 issue of *Foreign Affairs* contained an attack by Stanley Hoffman on balance-of-power theories such as those proposed by Henry Kissinger. Hoffman's purpose was to denounce the equilibrium model of five superstates (the United States, the Soviet Union, China, Japan and the European Economic Community).

> To use Raymond Aron's terms, the balance of power is a model of "strategic diplomatic behaviour." The essence of international relations is seen as a contest of states on a chessboard, on which the players try to maximise their power at each other's expense, and on which the possibility of war makes military potential and might the chief criterion of power. This view still fits much of the "game of nations," for it follows from the logic of a decentralised milieu, whatever the specific nature of the units or the social and economic systems which they embody.

Hoffman goes on to assert that this model is invalid, since it underestimates the predominance of the United States and the Soviet Union in nuclear equipment. Thus, he concludes that the chessboard image is inappropriate to the analysis of international relations.

It would be surprising if this abundant use of chess imagery had not found its enthusiasts in the military complex. And indeed it has. In the late eighteenth century the Duke of Brunswick was made head of the Prussian armies. He was viewed with great favor by Frederick the Great, who dispatched to him numerous young gentlemen to be instructed in military doctrine. The Duke instructed his master of pages, Herr Helwig, to produce a suitable and not too unpleasant mode of instruction. Helwig came up with the first modern war game:

> The idea came to me . . . of rendering sensible, not to say palpable, a few principles and rules of the military art . . . to pages of the Duke . . . and those young noblemen destined some day for military service. Independently of this objective my secondary one was to offer . . . an agreeable recreation by laying before them a game which, at first sight, presented different objects and operations, and which depended upon nothing but the rules and combinations made up by the players. The first thought which presented itself to my mind was that the learning of my game ought not to be burdened with too many details if it was to fulfill its mission. . . . I should achieve my objective in the quickest way if I took for its basis the game of chess . . . my idea was to adapt the game of chess to my own game . . .[5]

Helwig made a board of 1666 squares, colored according to geographical particularities. The pieces were modeled on chess pieces, receiving values according to the army of the time (since the original chess pieces were probably based on the state of the Indian army in the first century A.D.).[6]

"I was not deceived in my expectations," Helwig wrote, "and experience confirmed the wisdom of my judgment, for chess players were the first to welcome my invention; they found it a source of great amusement, and they set to work to make it better known." The Prussian General von der Goltz was not so enthusiastic— "This war game is a bad product of the refined military education of the period, which had piled up so many difficulties that it was incapable of taking a step in advance."

Despite such animadversions the genie was out of the bottle. Every staff college could boast of its war game— and by the early twentieth century most nurseries their boxes of Attack and Tri-tactics. Many of the battles of World War I were rehearsed in war games. After Versailles the German military, bereft for a time of actual troops, had to rely on war games. The invasion of Czechoslovakia was "gamed" in advance. The Germans also simulated invasions of the Ukraine and of England. The Japanese were also enthusiasts: "Late in 1941 Cinc Combined Fleet ordered all Fleet commanders and their key staff members to Tokyo for further war games. . . . On September 2 the final and most important games started . . . the details of a surprise raid on Pearl Harbor."

After the Second World War the United States took the lead. By the seventies over sixty organizations were interested in or engaged in war-gaming. In addition, STAG (United States Army Strategy and Tactics Analysis Group) estimates that of the more than two hundred organizations engaged in analysis in support of military decision-making, about one quarter of approximately three thousand projects per year utilize some war-gaming techniques.

All war games must, in the last analysis, ascribe certain behavior patterns to the "enemy." The war-gamer is in the position of having to define, within the limits of his knowledge, what he imagines the enemy's intentions are. Even minimax calculations of a zero-sum games' model imply some opinion of what the opposition might regard as minimum and maximum benefit.

The chess model assumes this knowledge, and so do war games that follow in its path. Chess is, after all, a game played on a one-to-one basis, in the sight of both parties, with parity of intention and with equality of forces. Its operation is one of initiative and response and counterinitiative. Although one or other of the players may devise a strategy that is difficult to analyze, it is always assumed that the object will become clear, as the player nears his objective of mating his opponent, and as the opponent comprehends that plan. The players are, in short, playing the same game.

At some levels this "chess matrix" can be transferred to the military or diplomatic plane, but the matrix still assumes, within certain limits, parity of intention and parity of means. Scott Boorman confronts the dangers of this position in his book *The Protracted Game*,[7] a *wei-chi* interpretation of Maoist revolutionary strategy. (*Wei-chi* is the Chinese name for the game more commonly known as Go.) As he remarks in his intoduction, "The value and validity of analysis of a military strategy employed at a given place and time are in great part determined by the strategic preconceptions of the analyst, by his criteria for assessing the importance and the correctness of a given strategic decision."

Boorman goes on to discuss Chinese strategy, which "abounds in paradoxes when judged by the standards of conventional Western military doctrine—its use of fluid operational methods and yet its reliance upon relatively stable base areas; its emphasis on efficiency and yet its tolerance of protraction; its delight in complexity in contrast to the simplicity of Western warfare." He suggests that Chinese strategy can in fact be best distinguished by reference to the game of *wei-chi*, and he proceeds at some length to do so.

But Boorman makes a mistake in his efforts to show that Western analysts must think themselves into the strategies and tactics of *wei-chi* to understand Chinese intentions and maneuvers. For Boorman, it is a question of counterposing Western to Eastern traditions, rather than bourgeois war to people's war. As a matter of fact chess is in origin an Eastern game; and the guerrilla warfare he discusses has emerged in the West. Chess can provide a very inadequate model of relations between similarly organized hierarchical states but is completely inapplicable to revolutionary civil war. *Wei-chi* is probably only a little bit better in this respect, since it too tends to start from some equivalence of position, at least in the sense that the two players are at the same game, with the same rules. This is never true of revolutionary civil war.

It is intriguing to speculate that 1972 was a year in which the major Communist powers, for their own reasons, were prepared to play the same game as Nixon, giving a strictly limited validity to Kissinger-type game theory. Now, chess may have some lessons for economic planning and conventional war and diplomacy—even though this is rare. But it has none for revolutionary struggle on the national and international plane, and this is where the Russian zealots for the game in the twenties made their mistake. Ultimately the antagonism and incomparability of United States imperialism on the one side and Russia and China as postrevolutionary states on the other will undermine any application of game theory to their relations with each other, just as the Vietnamese struggle invalidated it in Indochina.

No game model, such as chess, can in the end tolerate the notion of total contradiction, since all games accept the idea of rules. The subversive force is not the cheat. He accepts the rules in so far as he distorts them, within their terms. The subversive is the person who refuses to accept the rules at all. You cannot cheat at chess, but you can refuse to play it. The ultimate foolishness, of such people as the war-game planners, is to expect that everyone will play by the same rules with the same intentions as themselves. The game of chess is not, as I have tried to stress in this book, part of normal social reality. Symbolic meanings are not amenable to exact transliteration.

CHAPTER SEVEN

Chess and Life

PART ONE: ROBERT FISCHER

Do you ever worry that concentration on just one side of your character might have been a mistake?

I try to broaden myself. I read quite a bit. But it is a problem, because you're kind of out of touch with real life, being a chess player—not having to go to work and deal with people on that level. I've thought of giving it up off and on, but I always considered: what else could I do?

—JAMES BURKE and ROBERT FISCHER[1]

Chess is life.—ROBERT FISCHER

On June 2, 1972, Boris Spassky arrived in Reykjavik, Iceland, to defend the world championship against Bobby Fischer. From that day to September 1, the chess match and concomitant uproar were *the* major spectacle taking place in the world.[2] On September 1 Fischer won the twenty-first game and thus the championship by 12½ to

8½. It happens from time to time that world interest in an event or a pseudo event that would normally be of only marginal interest to many erupts with an intensity that retrospectively is almost impossible to credit.[3] As always with such spectacles, they seem unforgettable; but soon they are forgotten.

An acquaintance working in a West London factory at the time said that frequent—occasionally violent—altercations would break out among workers disputing the nature of the poisoned pawn: the canteen was in an uproar over the merits and demerits of each player's performance. He confirmed the supposition, which was that nearly all the people involved had normally no interest in chess, nor the slightest interest in pretending that they had.

Similar scenes were enacted all over the world. In the United States public television ran interminable commentaries on the match, bizarre parodies of the normal desiderata of modern sports reporting. The moves were relayed by a reporter from Iceland to the New York offices of a wire service. From there the move was reported by telephone to the Albany studio of New York Channel 13. Finally, the commentators—notably Shelby Lyman—would adjust the large board in conformity with the latest information. To fill out the inevitable *longueurs*, the commentators would speculate on the moves that might be made, evaluate the moves that had already been made and suggest the moves they might like to make themselves. It was quite common at that time to find nonplayers following the commentaries with grim concentration, as though it was not enough that they should know who had won the game but that protracted suspense in following the meaningless operations of that game was necessary for full enjoyment.

There were all the trappings of spectacular drama:[4]

THE SETTING. Iceland, land of the midnight sun, covered with lava and surrounded by fish.

THE CHORUS. A vast conglomeration of chess masters, chess fans, citizens of Iceland and journalists of the world. From June 2, the arrival of Spassky, to July 11, the date of the first game, these journalists have very little to do, except wait for Fischer to arrive, interview experts and Icelandic citizens and one another. Thus, the normal equation: low input of fact + high quotient of audience interest = high output of rubbish. There are sharp gradings of journalistic stature and required rhetoric. There are superpundits, largely grandmasters like Gligoric; pundits first-class, like Arthur Koestler; mere pundits, such as the regular chess commentators; mere journalists, innumerable.

BIT PLAYERS. There are the *harried officials* who "hope only for first-class chess." These include Max Euwe, exworld champion and leading representative of FIDE, the international chess organization and Lothar Schmid, the main referee. Other bit players include William Lombardy, the obese Catholic priest, who is Fischer's second; "stocky, tough, loquacious" Fred Cramer, Vice-President of the American Chess Federation and chief spokesman for Fischer; the "enigmatic" Krogius, who is Spassky's counselor in matters of psychology; Chester Fox, the promoter who hopes to film the proceedings; and, in a bit of overwriting, John Collins, a paraplegic in a wheelchair who developed the youthful Fischer's chess talents.

MAIN PLAYERS. Boris Spassky, polite Russian and "perfect gentleman"; Bobby Fischer, unpredictable, moody, erratic, childish, childlike, sulky, overweening, arrogant, boastful, nose-picking, ear-gouging, sleepless, neurotic, obsessed, driven, monstrous challenger.

THE AUDIENCE. Worldwide.

EXPECTATIONS OF AUDIENCE. Ritual struggle; decency versus daemonism; United States versus the Soviet Union; the collective brains of Soviet chessdom versus the loner from Brooklyn; destruction of Spassky versus psychotic breakdown of Fischer; victory versus defeat.

KITSCH SYMBOLISM. "Symbolic" battle of minds; nastiness versus niceness; mathematical infinity of possibility versus the judgment of a single brain. And, of course, cosmic political drama: the United States versus the Soviet Union; the boy from Brooklyn versus the potent resources of the Asian mind; our brain against theirs.

THE OPERATIC DRAMA. Much coming and going in the early acts. Will Fischer come to Iceland? The chorus speculates about this at great length. There are many fine contributions from individual members of the cast. In *recitativo* it is revealed that Fischer wants more money. Breathless messengers arrive on stage with news that he is coming. Fresh messengers announce that he is not. A moving song from Spassky in which he says that he hopes only for good chess. Comical stage "business" after this in which Spassky announces that he would like to kick Fischer in the behind. At the end of the first act a general chorus by all, in which it is agreed that the ways of man are strange and the future wrapped in darkness.

ACT TWO. A splendid opening scene in which Fischer arrives. The stage is covered with hurrying figures, chanting with pleasure, setting up cameras, seeking to

obtain interviews with Fischer. All congregate for the
Opening Ceremony and await the dramatic entry of the
Hero-Villain. He does not appear. He is asleep. Grand-
Master Geller (Spassky's second) sings a magnificent
aria protesting Fischer's absence and other lapses "in
violation of the Amsterdam agreement and FIDE rules
and contradictory to his (Euwe's) own letter from May
5, 1972." This aria melts into a duet with Cramer, who
opens with "We wish to understand more of the intent
and purpose of such a statement, and to support the
great event here in Iceland in all reasonable ways." Tension builds up: the Russians demand apologies, insist on
observance of rules. Much complicated *recitativo*, as
from Cramer—"Euwe's condemnation of Bobby is going
to look pretty silly to our grandchildren when they read
the book of games. This match is going to be a very elegant event." He says that Bobby is having his pants
pressed. However the chorus is full of gloom and fore-
boding again—"the ways of man are strange"—but they
break off as a messenger rushes in with the news that the
Hero has written to Spassky. The whole chorus gathers
to hear the messenger's report of this brilliant letter:

> DEAR BORIS, Please accept my sincerest apology
> . . . disrespectful behavior . . . petty dispute over
> money . . . offended you and your country . . .
> thousands of chess fans round the world and espe-
> cially to the millions of fans and many friends I have
> in the United States . . . first game to be forfeited
> to you . . . tremendous disadvantage . . . in other
> words I must win *three!* games without losses, just to
> obtain the position you would have at the beginning
> of the match . . . don't believe the world's champion

desires such an advantage . . . I know you to be a sportsman and a gentleman, and I am looking forward to some exciting chess games with you.

All conclude that the Hero has scored a great tactical triumph by this letter. The act concludes on a note of hope.

ACT THREE. Some incidental events at the start to keep the audience on its toes. Fischer loses the first game to Spassky. The chorus wisely comments that he has turned a drawn game into a lost one by a grave blunder on the twenty-ninth move. Fischer now complains about the television cameras, and fails to appear for the second game. He forfeits it. Renewed anxiety on the part of the chorus: messengers report that Dr. Kissinger has spoken by telephone to Fischer, encouraging him to play. Important business now takes place off stage, as the two main characters do battle in the third game in a small room. Fischer wins a great victory. Both now return to the main stage for the rest of the drama. They do more or less continual battle, amid much excited comment from the chorus. By the end of the tenth game the chorus has decided who will win, since Fischer leads by 6½ to 3½; it wisely comments that Spassky is "a broken man"; messengers report that he looks worried and ill. However Spassky wins the eleventh game, allowing the chorus the "bowed but unbroken" song it has been keenly rehearsing. This interminable chant is kept up till the twenty-first game, which Fischer wins and which wins him the championship. All gather on stage for a victory feast and final celebration. Some confusing asides to the audience that "Spassky will defect, and fears to return to the Soviet Union." These are discounted by more knowledgeable members of the cast. In the course of a final song, in which all join and Fischer is hailed as the greatest champion ever and the money and fame that await him in his native land are described, all exit. The stage is rapidly cleared and readied for the next performance, which has a sturdy cast of Icelandic and British trawlermen.

This brief review does not do justice to the whole spectacle. For example, the splendid episode during the seventeenth game when the Russians claimed that the special chair that Fischer had imported had a fiendish device with chemical, electronic or hypnotic properties which were sapping Spassky's strength. The chair was dismantled amid jocular comment from the cast to reveal two dead flies. Other critics might care to make more of the language of the messengers' speeches; as for example Mary Kenny in the London *Evening Standard:* "It had appeared like temperamental behaviour; now we know it was all part of Bobby's deadly plan for Spassky's psychological destruction: the strategy to wear the Russian down to a pulp of frayed nerves and raw tension, the better that he could move in for the viperous kill." Others again might comment on the huge enthusiasm for chess that sprang up, with sales of chess sets breaking all records and people predicting that chess would become *the* leisure pastime of the people. This closely paralleled the chess mania that swept the United States in the late 1850s, when Morphy played his famous games in Europe. "As the enthusiasm grew," reported *Brentano's Chess Monthly* at the time, "we began to discover, to our surprise, that nearly everyone we knew either were chess players or were going to learn to be; it became all at once 'a big thing' to be a player of that game in which our countryman was beating all creation, and he who could best explain the ins and outs of the full reports of Morphy's various matches which appeared in the *Herald* and other city papers was the centre of the attraction in every place of public resort."[5]

The Match of the Century. . . . It passed the time for people in the July and August of 1972. It receded in the face of Kissinger's "peace is at hand" speech and the Nixon-McGovern election campaign.

There are various famous and informative scenes in Fischer's life: the Game of the Century victory over Byrne, when Fischer was thirteen, with the sacrifice of his Queen on the seventeenth move; the acquisition of the U.S. Junior Championship in the same year; and the acquisition of the United States Championship at the age of fourteen. There was his attack on the Russians, following his disastrous performance in the Candidates tournament in 1962. Finally there was his unparalleled string of victories in 1970 and 1971 when, in three major tournaments he won 57 games, drew 22 and lost only 3. These were the staggering years in which he did "destroy"—to use a word much in Fischer's mouth—his opponents and inflict inconceivable losses on them.

There is also, throughout his playing career, the gradual construction of the Fischer myth: the moody and arrogant loner, obsessed only with chess, elusive, unapproachable. Some have claimed that much of this *is* myth; for example, the *Life* magazine reporter who accompanied Fischer to Iceland painted a glowing portrait of a healthy lad, keen on girls, never happier than when sitting down to a bracing platter of sizzled sheep's head

with an Icelandic family, and much elated to hear of
President Nixon's approval of his triumph.[6]

Let us run a zigzag track through Fischer's life and see
if we can gradually compose a portrait.

Fischer was born in Chicago in 1943. His father was a
physicist and his mother a registered nurse and school-
teacher. He has one older sister. His parents were divorced when he was a baby, and his mother took the
family to California, to Arizona, and finally to Brooklyn,
New York. Fischer's father seems to have left the country soon after Fischer was born. The family was run by
Mrs. Fischer. Her first name is Regina, the Latin word
for "Queen."

Fischer began to play chess at the age of six. "My sister bought me a set at a candy store and taught me the
moves," he remarked to Ralph Ginzburg in an interesting and important interview he gave in 1961.[7] In another interview ten years later, he said:

> I just found I had more of a feel for the game, more
> of a knack for winning than others had. I liked
> games; I was playing a lot of board games at home.
> We had Pachisi, Monopoly and all these board games,
> Chinese chequers and what-not, but I kept hearing
> the hardest game was chess, so I finally persuaded my
> mother to give me that. They thought it would be too
> advanced for me, but they finally got me a set, and
> that is the game I concentrated on from then on. . . .
> I played a little with my sister, but she wasn't too in-
> terested, so then I started playing games with myself.
> I would make the white moves and the black moves,
> and then I would just play through the whole game.
> My mother started to get worried that it wasn't too

healthy playing chess by myself, so she got me some opponents, local kids. I started getting some lessons from a player in the Brooklyn chess club, and that is when I started to advance.[8]

Fischer has remarked that about this time he liked to walk around parks, see old men poring over chess tables and then move in and "crush them." By the age of fifteen he had won the United States Championship and become an international grand master.[9]

> After that I quit school [he told Ginzburg]. You don't learn anything in school. It's just a waste of time. You lug around books and all and do homework. They give too much homework. You shouldn't be doing homework. Nobody's interested in it. The teachers are stupid. They shouldn't have women in there. They don't know how to teach. And they shouldn't make anyone go to school. You don't want to go, you don't go, that's all. It's ridiculous. I don't remember one thing I learned in school. I don't listen to weakies. My two and a half years in Erasmus High I wasted. You have to mix with all those stupid kids. The teachers are even stupider than the kids. They talk down to the kids. Half of them are crazy. If they'd have let me, I would have quit before I was sixteen.

"How did your mother feel about that?" asked Ginzburg. "She and I just don't see eye to eye together. She's a square. She keeps telling me that I'm too interested in chess, that I should get friends outside of chess, that I should finish high school and all that nonsense. She keeps in my hair and I don't like people in my hair, you know, so I had to get rid of her."

"You mean she moved out of the Brooklyn apartment you lived in?"

"Yeh, she moved in with her girl friend in the Bronx, and I kept the apartment. But right now she's away on this trip with those people (the pacifists) for about eight months. I don't have anything to do with her."

Mrs. Fischer is, by all accounts, a strong-willed woman. She comes from a Jewish family in Switzerland, is a woman of wide culture and determined personality. Fischer fans tend to treat her unkindly—"She was a dominating, ambitious woman" (C. H. O'D. Alexander); "His mother was an adolescent's nightmare" (Thomas Powers in *Rolling Stone*). One could take this as the ambivalence of chess players toward the mother figure; in fact what Mrs. Fischer did was to attempt to further her son's chess career by dramatic activities. She would rise with what Powers called "shrill" questions at meetings of the U.S. Chess Federation. In the summer of 1960 she chained herself to the White House gate to protest the government's refusal to send a chess team to East Germany. She once tried to sell Bobby Fischer Chess Wallets. In 1961 she joined in a march across Europe to Moscow as part of a pacifist antiwar demonstration. Her daughter says that "she is something of a professional crusader," evidently for liberal causes. She has been photographed carrying banners saying "End Jim Crow," and recently one saying "I am an American protesting the war in Vietnam." The first line of this last banner was so written as to say "I A M A N." She has since remarried and now lives in England.

Ginzburg made the point to Fischer that his mother seemed to have helped him in his chess career: "I was under the impression that she had a great deal to do with the success of your career. . . ." "Yeh," answered Fischer, "but she doesn't know what she's doing. She ought to keep out of chess." Thus, at the age of sixteen or seventeen Fischer was completely without family ties. For a while after his mother moved out, she paid his rent, food and clothing bills; but as soon as he could afford it, he stopped taking the money.

He became a professional chess player, and his remarks to Ginzburg about his trade are interesting: "Reshevsky and I are the only ones in America who try. We don't make much. The other masters have outside jobs. Like, Rossolimo, he drives a cab. Evans, he works for the movies. The Russians, they get money from the government. We have to depend on tournament prizes. And they're lousy. Maybe a couple of hundred bucks. Millionaires back this game but they're all cheap. Look what they do for golf: thirty thousand dollars for a tournament is nothing. But for chess they give a thousand or two, and they think it's a big deal. The tournament has to be named after them, everybody has to bow down to them, play when they want, everything for a couple of thousand dollars, which is nothing to them anyhow. They take it off their income tax. These people are cheap. It's ridiculous." (Ginzburg later estimated that at that time Fischer was making about $5,000 a year out of chess.)

Paul Marshall, Fischer's lawyer in the Reykjavik match, remarked to one interviewer, "You've got to remember two things. First, Bobby never made any money in his life. Everyone who dealt with him when he was fourteen, fifteen used him. If there was any money to be made they took it. They'd call him up and say, 'Come on out here, we'll pay your bills, we'll give you a couple of bucks on the side.' And when it was over, they'd stick him with a huge hotel bill. Here's a fifteen-year-old kid with no money, all alone, a huge bill, crying."

Thus a great many of Fischer's social fantasies have to do with financial success commensurate with his estimate of the value of chess. Ginzburg asked him what he would do if he won the World Championship: "First of all I'll make a tour of the whole world, giving exhibitions. I'll charge unprecedented prices. I'll set new standards. I'll make them pay thousands. Then I'll come home on a luxury liner. First class. I'll have a tuxedo made for me in England to wear to dinner. When I come home I'll write a couple of chess books and start to reorganize the whole game. I'll have my own club. The Bobby Fischer —uh, the Robert J. Fischer Chess Club. Tournaments in full dress. No bums in there. You're gonna have to be over eighteen to get in, unless, like, you have special permission because you have, like, special talent. It'll be in a part of the city that's still decent, like the Upper East Side. And I'll hold big international tournaments in my club, with big cash prizes. And I'm going to kick all the millionaires out of chess, unless they kick in more money. Then I'll buy a car so I don't have to take the subway anymore. That subway makes me sick. . . . Then I'll build me a house. I don't know where, but it won't be in Greenwich Village. They're all dirty, filthy animals down there. . . ."

It was evident that Fischer had a low estimate of women. Ginzburg remarked that Lisa Lane, U.S. Women's Chess Champion, had said that Fischer was the greatest player alive. "That statement is accurate," answered Fischer, "but Lisa really wouldn't be in a position to know. They're all weak, all women. They're stupid compared to men. They shouldn't play chess, you know. They're like beginners. They lose every single game against a man. There isn't a woman player in the world I can't give knight odds to and still beat."

Secondly, Fischer has been, and certainly still was at the time of the Reykjavik match, obsessed with appearance, and with the gaze of the others. Up until about the age of fourteen or fifteen Fischer would play dressed in sneakers, jeans and T-shirt. From sixteen on, this was all changed. He decided that people were not paying enough respect, so he began to dress smartly. He would have his suits custom-made all over the world. "Do you have any objection to ready-made clothes?" asked Ginzburg. "Oh, I wouldn't touch them. I have my shoes made to order, my shirts, everything. . . . I'd like to be one of the Ten Best Dressed Men." He disliked American millionaires because "they dress like slobs." At one point Fischer had been thinking of learning judo, but he found the gymnasiums too low-class, "with too much riffraff and no place to put your clothes." Generalizing his interest, he said that "they say you can tell the decline of a nation when the people begin to lose interest in their clothes. Nowadays if you're dressed up, people think you are a dandy. In the olden days the most virile men were the men who dressed the best."

But although Fischer disliked American millionaires "because they dress casually and all, they're, like, afraid to be looked at," he seems to have a similar aversion. "You travel around the city mainly by subway?" "Unfortunately, yes. It's dirty. Kids there see I have nice shoes on so they try to step on them on purpose. People come in there in their work clothes and all, people come charging in like animals, it's terrible. People sitting and staring directly across the aisles at you, it's barbaric." Fischer's dislike of being looked at, or "spied on," came to a head in Iceland, with the interminable dispute over the film cameras in the tournament hall. First he said they might be noisy. They were made silent. Then he said they might distract him by their presence. They were concealed. Finally he exploded. "I *know* they're there, whether I can see them or not," he shouted. So the match, in direct contradiction of his own financial interests, was not filmed. We saw, in the case of other chess masters, that they have an exhibitionist urge and partook in distressing incidents involving clothes. Morphy believed there was a conspiracy to steal his garments; Torre took all his clothes off in a bus. Fischer's motivations are partly indicated in one response to Ginzburg: "When it was a game played by aristocrats it had more, like, you know, dignity to it. When they used to have the clubs, like, no women were allowed and everybody went in dressed in a suit, a tie, like gentlemen, you know. Now kids come running in in their sneakers—even in the best chess club—and they've got women in there. . . ."

"Am I correct in surmising that there are quite a number of Jews in the upper echelons of chess?"

"Yeah, there are too many Jews in chess. They seem to have taken away the class of the game. They don't seem to dress so nicely, you know. That's what I don't like."

"You're Jewish, aren't you?"

"Part Jewish. My mother is Jewish."

At the conclusion of their interview in 1961, Ginzburg took Fischer back to Bedford-Stuyvesant (a neighborhood about as different from the Upper East Side as it is possible to be) and stopped off on the way "at a posh espresso house for a bite to eat. Bobby ordered a pecan cream pie, a side order of butter cookies, and an elaborate frozen pineapple drink. When he had finished his pie, I mentioned that the place was reputed to be owned and operated by homosexuals. Bobby was horrified and eyed the waiters narrowly. 'Gee, you'd think the place would die off with a reputation like that.' He turned his attention to his drink. 'Maybe they put something in here. I better not drink it.' He didn't touch it again. Nor did he eat any more of his cookies." If one argues, as Fine and Reider have done, that the game has an element of sublimated homosexuality in it, then Ginzburg's news about the ownership of the café might well induce in Fischer some feeling of alarm and paranoia at the direct confrontation with an impulse normally disarmed in play.

Fischer's chess career in the sixties was punctuated by rows and by withdrawals from championship chess. In 1960 he ended thirteenth in the Buenos Aires tournament, which one commentator calls "a still inexplicable result." In 1961 he forfeited a match with Reshevsky rather than concede what he considered to be a point of principle. In 1962 he had a major triumph in the Interzonal in Stockholm, but this was followed by a poor performance in the Candidates Tournament (for a shot at the world championship). He came only fourth, and immediately lashed out with his attack on the Russians for "fixing world chess." There was some truth in his attack, but experts consider his performance at Curaçao to have been poor anyway. Fischer withdrew from international chess for two years. Between 1965 and 1967 he once again played successful top-level chess, but in the Interzonal (prelude to the candidates round) at Sussex in 1967 he once again refused to concede on "a point of principle" and withdrew from the tournament in which he held a most commanding position. He partially withdrew from chess for two years. In 1970 he commenced the dazzling run of successes that culminated in Reykjavik in 1972.

There is one other point to be made about his general conduct during these years—namely, his extraordinary aggressiveness. Lay people do not always realize that chess is fundamentally an aggressive game, no matter that the player conducts himself with decorum and makes a show of shaking hands with his opponent. But with Fischer there is no concealment. He refers to "weakies." He shouts "Smash," "Crunch," "Bam," as he plays games on his pocket set, and slaughters again in retrospect his former opponents. "I like to see their ego crumble," he told an audience of millions, on the Cavett show, as he discussed the pleasures of victory. Since at least 1961 he has considered himself to be the greatest player in the world, and with this self-regard has gone a certain grandioseness in assessing the meaning of the world championship: "This is where it's at," he said just before he went to Reykjavik. "It's the apex of my whole life, taking on this Spassky. This is really the big match. This is for everything. This is for the title. If I don't win, it's not going to be easy to get up to again. This little thing between me and Spassky, it's a microcosm of the whole world political situation. They always suggest that the two world leaders should fight it out hand to hand, and this is the kind of thing that we are doing—not with bombs, but battling it out over the board."

It takes no great perception to remark the enormous effect his fatherless youth, his upbringing by his mother and their later break must have had on his character. Given innate talent, his submersion in chess is scarcely surprising, and the satisfactions of the sublimation offered by the family drama conducted on the board very signal. In his book *The Champions*, Peter Fuller explains the "inexplicable" defeat at Buenos Aires by pointing out that it occurred just after Regina Fischer's departure from the Brooklyn flat. Fuller also suggests, apropos the famous Queen's sacrifice in the Game of the Century match against Byrne, that the sacrifice was of the Queen within himself, feminine identification, that is, a denial of his own homosexuality, caused by identification with Regina; fitting in with persecution fears and paranoia which Freud saw as disguised defenses against homosexuality. The obsession with money and ritualistic observance of "form" coincides with the anal-obsessive aspect of his character.

Throughout the sixties Fischer moved to the right in his reverence for authority symbols. He became close to (though apparently never an actual member of) a small fundamentalist sect called the World Church of God, which observes Jewish holidays. Fischer still will not play on the Sabbath. According to one report, when he was in training at Grossinger's for the 1972 championship he would listen every night at ten past ten to "Church of the Air," a program vague on theology and precise on questions of right and wrong. According to an elder of the Church of God, Fischer was considerably more correct in his adherence to sect rules than many who were actually members.

No player has ever been such a walking advertisement for the Freudian interpretation of chess, and few players have ever expressed with such eloquence their sense that the game has come down in the world, that it is played in tacky clubs with no class. Fischer longs for a return to the days of Parsloe's and the patronage of the European aristocracy. ("I admire the aristocrats. You know, the millionaires, except they're millionaires the way millionaires ought to be, not the way millionaires are. They're the European millionaires.") He has fought for a return to this former status. And after his triumph in Iceland he was on the verge of success. Aides of Fischer estimated to journalists that side offers and contracts to Fischer in the year after the victory could be as valuable as ten million dollars. He was offered a $1.4 million contract by the Hilton Motel chain for a match at Las Vegas—of all places!—with Fischer retaining subsidiary rights. He could have cleared two million dollars. Warners' wanted him to do a recording called "How to Play Chess." It would have taken him little time, and they offered $100,000 against royalties. New York publishers pursued him with offers of up to $500,000 for a book on the championship. The glittering dream he painted to Ginzburg in 1961 could have come absolutely true. He could have made millions in a year, when the public interest was at its peak.

Yet Fischer turned down every offer. He went into

seclusion on the West Coast near the site of the World Church of God and then in Denver. There are reports that he is disillusioned with the World Church, to which he was a contributor. Even the odd sponsored tournament will not earn the vast sums that were available to him in late 1972 and early 1973. The point is that money is not Fischer's gratification, even though he may propose gigantic sums and be uncompromising about them. (It is unclear whether he ever actually collected Jim Slater's famous cash offer, which got the Iceland match off the ground.) Fischer's gratification is at the chessboard. At a fundamental level, huge commercial success may collide with his real feelings about the game as a "pure" activity uncontaminated by the baser aspects of life. Thus, he will raise the stakes in every situation to a point that makes one suspect that he actually *wants* the terms to be turned down.

Yet his fantasy picture of a chess champion's life collides with the reality of cheap tournaments and cheaper clubs. He knows that chess is not "work," and he is "out of touch with real life," as he put it in 1972. But as he also said, "What else could I do?" Uniquely Fischer represents the splendors and miseries of the chess player. As Frank Brady wrote, "The initiated [chess players] are promised the destiny of having to live a monk-like existence and know more rejection than any artist ever has, struggling to be known and accepted." He added, "Chess is a sport—a violent sport. . . . Of course, one intriguing aspect of the game that does imply artistic connotations is the actual geometric patterns and variations of the actual setup of the pieces, and the combinative, tactical, strategic and positional sense. It's a sad expression though—somewhat like religious art. It's not very gay. If anything, it's a struggle."

Brady stresses one all-important point. If any activity is akin to that of the chess player, it must be the artist's, both in the aesthetic sense, and in the social context, in terms of value placed on one's activity by the community. Yet the artist can feel he is producing something of value, and his productions can be appropriated by the middle and upper classes. His "work" is recognized and is rewarded accordingly. The artist may see this as a betrayal, even if it is a necessary one; and an avant-garde artist may be constantly alert to the ironies of his position—challenging bourgeois conceptions, yet being supported by the bourgeoisie. Thus is his activity different from chess, a purer, harsher activity with much more infrequent sanctions from society.

There is one artist who was also a first-class chess player, and who devoted his life to a meditation on what exactly "useful art" was; what the relation of an artist was to the class that supported him; how much of culture was playful irrelevance—Marcel Duchamp.

PART TWO: MARCEL DUCHAMP

Chess has no social purpose. That, above all, is important.—MARCEL DUCHAMP

Irony is a playful way of accepting something. Mine is the irony of indifference. It is a "meta-irony."—MARCEL DUCHAMP

Marcel Duchamp (1887–1968) was a rationalist. His mode was irony. He had no great reverence for art. Of Picasso he remarked sarcastically that "every now and then the world looks for an individual on whom to rely blindly—such worship is comparable to a religious appeal and goes beyond reasoning. Thousands today in search of supernatural emotion turn to Picasso, who never lets them down." Duchamp's original affinity was for the Dada painters and poets, who in the years during and after the First World War strove to devalue the work of art, to demystify "artistic" activity. In the spirit of this movement Duchamp put mustachios on the Mona Lisa and sent a urinal along to an exhibition, entitled "Fountain." It was Duchamp who invented "ready-mades," who introduced the chance happening into art, who invented kinetic art. When one reviews the history of the twentieth-century avant-garde, Duchamp stands at its center—ironic and intelligent. For forty years he was a top-class chess player. He shuttled between Paris and New York for half a century from the end of the First World War, never dramatically rich, never outrageously poor. "I live the life of a restaurant waiter," he remarked to one person; to another, with some complacency, he said, "I didn't have a wife, a child, any baggage you see. People were always asking me how I lived, but one never knows. One gets along. Life goes on just the same." Duchamp's basic motive in life was the avoidance of just such encumbrances; and beyond this the kind of encumbrance that "an artist" might proclaim as necessary—faithfulness to his "mission," or to his "vision" or his "duty to society" or something of that sort. As early as 1910—two years before his "Nude Descending a Staircase" was exhibited at the Armory show in New York and became for many Americans the definition of what modern art was about—Duchamp made this impression on one observer:

> Though very much detached from the conventions of his epoch, he had not yet found his mode of expression, and this gave him a kind of disgust with work and an ineptitude for life. Under an appearance of almost romantic timidity, he possessed an exacting dialectical mind, in love with philosophical speculations and absolute conclusions. He enclosed himself in the solitude of his studio at Neuilly, keeping in touch with only a few friends. By a discipline that was almost Jansenist and mystical, he suppressed every impulse, every desire to create, suppressed all joy in creating, and to avoid the danger of a routine reminiscence or reflex, forced himself to a rule of conduct directly counter to the natural.

The same observer saw him in New York, after Duchamp had been rejected for service as unfit in 1914.

> We had found Marcel Duchamp perfectly adapted to the violent rhythm of New York. He was the hero of the artists and intellectuals, and of the young ladies who frequented these circles. Leaving his almost monastic isolation, he flung himself into orgies of drunkenness and every other excess. But in a life of license as of asceticism he preserved his consciousness of purpose; extravagant as his gestures sometimes seemed, they were perfectly adequate to his experimental study of a personality disengaged from the normal contingencies of human life. . . . In art he

was interested only in finding new formulas with which to assault the tradition of the picture and of painting; despite the pitiless pessimism of his mind, he was personally delightful with his jolly ironies. . . . Utterly logical, he soon declared his intention of renouncing all artistic production. And if he continued to busy himself with his great work in glass, "The Bride Stripped Bare by Her Bachelors, Even," to which for two years he had been devoting such meticulous care, it was because it had been purchased prior to completion. He was almost happy when it was cracked in moving. As to painting, he kept his word, he never again touched a brush. But at long intervals he did work on certain strange objects or machines, strictly useless and antiaesthetic. . . . He drugged himself on chess, playing night and day like a professional.[10]

There was, really coming out of French nineteenth-century bohemianism, a strong emphasis on the necessity for the artist's personality as much as his work to be an affront to bourgeois canons of behavior. The most famous example was Jarry, author of *Ubu Roi*. A number of the Dadaists and surrealists picked up this thread; the merciless criticism of all that exists had to be expressed in personal conduct and stance. *Nothing* must connect the artist to bourgeois reality, except the challenge presented by the artist.

Duchamp affected this attitude; his pose was not one of urgency, but one of nonchalance. "I think," he remarked once, "a picture dies after a few years like the man who made it. Afterward it is called the history of art. The history of art is something very different from aesthetics. For me the history of art is what remains of an epoch in a museum, but it's not probably the best of that epoch, and fundamentally it's probably the expression of mediocrity in that epoch, because the beautiful things have disappeared—because the public does not want to keep them." Then he added deprecatingly, "But this is philosophy." Yet Duchamp *was* interested in having his work preserved in museums, as the Arensberg Collection in Philadelphia attests. Despite his contempt for dealers and bourgeois patrons, he made successful interventions in this field himself. He never had much money, but he always had enough. Irony did not include starvation.

In 1921 he finished the famous picture known informally as the Large Glass and formally as "The Bride Stripped Bare by Her Bachelors, Even." The word "finished" is too definite. It took Duchamp five years to arrive at the form where he finally abandoned it, "Because," he said, "in the end you lose interest in it, so I didn't feel the need to finish it." And the actual content of the Large Glass, the work Duchamp took most seriously, before he abandoned the activity for chess? Arturo Schwartz, in his excellent book on Duchamp, describes it in these terms:

> As soon as we see the Large Glass as the diagram of a love-making machine its arrangement becomes clear: the male and female machines function separately and without any point of contact. Since the clockwork which was to have released the unhooking of the dress was not completed, the Bride (like the Nude who was not nude) was *not* stripped bare by her bachelors. More than that, the splashing reaches her only if reflected in a mirror, according to the well-

tested technique of *coitus interruptus,* which leaves her literally hanging in the air, halfway between the satisfaction that would bring about her downfall and the blossoming that would compensate for her frustration. Should Duchamp have revealed his pessimism so publicly? He would seem to me to leave only a simultaneous mechanism which in no way implies a spiritual or even a physical union: men and women acting upon each other *from a distance* and on separate planes, she the victim of her illusions, always keeping herself above the point of contact, while he, the prisoner of his instincts, is designed never to reach it. The result, in short, would be onanism for two.[11]

Duchamp abandoned this complex depiction of sterility, of total desentimentalism in 1921. It was his large major work for over twenty years. The intervening period he gave over obsessively to chess.

Duchamp had been taught chess by his brothers, at the same time as they taught him painting. There are some pictures by him of chess players dated around 1910. By the early twenties he was writing to friends, "It's a long time that I've been wanting to write to you. But I haven't been able to find the time: my attention is so completely absorbed in chess. I play night and day, and nothing interests me more than finding the right move . . . I like painting less and less."

So intense was his addiction that when he contracted a somewhat frivolous marriage with Lydia Levassor-Sarrazin in 1927 "he spent most of the one week they lived together studying chess problems, and his bride, in desperate retaliation, got up one night when he was asleep and glued the chess pieces to the board. They were divorced three months later."[12] Considering that she was, in one sense, immobilizing the components of the Oedipal drama, she is lucky to have sustained only the good fortune of divorce.

Duchamp's rationalization of his activity is interesting and explicit. He immersed himself in the game with a very conscious desire to find uselessness and unprofitable beauty. He also wanted to show that the old phrase *"bête comme un peintre"* ("stupid as a painter") was not true. As a friend said, "Marcel wanted to show that an artist's mind, if it wasn't corrupted by money or success, could equal the best in the field. He thought that, with its sensitivity to images and sensations, the artist's mind could do as well in chess as the scientific mind with its mathematical memory. But of course the memory boys were tougher and they had trained for it from an early age. Marcel started too late in life."

Nonetheless it must be emphasized that Duchamp was an extremely strong player. He played on the French team with Alekhine. He won several tournaments, including some New York club championships. In 1967 and 1968 he coached the United States team. At one point he was the best French player. Something of his attitude to the game can be gleaned from the interviews he gave to Pierre Cabanne toward the end of his life:

> CABANNE: Your passion for chess . . . ?
> DUCHAMP: It's not a serious matter, but it does exist.
> CABANNE: But I also noticed that this passion was specially great when you weren't painting.
> DUCHAMP: That's true.
> CABANNE: So I wondered whether, during those pe-

riods, the gestures directing the movements of pawns in space didn't give rise to imaginary creations—yes, I know you don't like that word—creations which in your eyes had as much value as the real creation of your pictures and further established a new plastic function in space.

DUCHAMP: In a certain sense, yes. A game of chess is a visual plastic thing, and if it isn't geometric in the static sense of the word, it is mechanical, since it moves; it's a drawing, it's mechanical reality. The pieces aren't pretty in themselves, any more than the form of the game, but what is pretty—if the word "pretty" can be used—is the movement. Well, it's mechanical—the way, for example, a Calder is mechanical. In chess there are some extremely important things in the domain of movement, but not in the visual domain. It is the imagining of the movement or of the gesture that makes the beauty in this case. It's completely in one's gray matter.

CABANNE: In short, there is in chess a gratuitous play of forms as opposed to the functional play of forms on the canvas.

DUCHAMP: Yes, completely. Although chess play is not gratuitous. There is choice.

CABANNE: But no intended purpose?

DUCHAMP: No, there is no social purpose. That above all is important.

CABANNE: Chess is the ideal work of art?

DUCHAMP: That could be. Also the milieu of chess players is far more sympathetic than that of artists. These people are completely cloudy, completely blinkered . . . madmen of a certain quality, the way an artist is supposed to be and isn't, in general. That's probably what interested me the most.

I was highly attracted to chess for forty or forty-
five years, then little by little my enthusiasm
lessened."[13]

There were three things really that interested him:
the beauty, the milieu and the uselessness. Lasker com-
mented that "Duchamp was a very strong player and a
marvelous opponent. He would always take risks in order
to play a beautiful game, rather than be cautious and
brutal to win." About the beauty of chess, Duchamp
made a number of references; to Truman Capote he
wrote, "Why isn't my chess playing an art activity? A
chess game is very plastic. You construct it. It's mechanical sculpture and with chess one creates beautiful problems and that beauty is made with the head and the
brains." And in an address to the New York State Chess
Association in 1952 he said, "I believe that every chess
player experiences a mixture of two aesthetic pleasures:
first, the abstract imagery akin to the poetic idea of writing; secondly, the sensuous pleasure of that ideographic
execution on the chessboard. From my close contact with
artists and chess players I have come to the conclusion
that while all artists are not chess players, all chess players are artists."

The uselessness had a great appeal to him. He said on
more than one occasion "Chess is purer, socially, than
painting, for you can't make money out of it." And his
playful desire to emphasize its utter nonutility came out
even in the book he wrote about chess—the only technical one avowedly useless even for players:

> CABANNE: In 1932 you wrote a work on chess which
> became a classic, called "The Opposition and Sister

Squares Reconciled." It's a marvelous, surrealist title.

DUCHAMP: The "Opposition" is a system that allows you to do such and such a thing. The "sister squares" are the same thing as the opposition, but it's a more recent invention, which was given a different name. Naturally the defenders of the old system were always wrangling with the defenders of the new one. I added "reconciled" because I had found a system that did away with the antithesis. But the end games in which it works would interest no chess player. That's the funny part. There are only two or three people in the world who have tried to do the same research as Halberstadt, who wrote the book with me, and myself. Even the chess champions don't read the book, since the problem it poses really comes up only once in a lifetime. They're end-game problems of possible games but so rare as to be nearly Utopian.

CABANNE: You always stayed in the conceptual domain.

DUCHAMP: Oh, yes, completely. It was neither common, nor utilitarian.

Yet there are further paradoxes to Duchamp. If he was the only great artist ever to be a strong chess player, he was one of the few strong players ever to be a keen gambler. As we have seen more than once, there has always been a curious attraction-repulsion between the two activities, the one nominally an affair of reason, the other a prostration to chance. But even if one points to the dice method of playing chess, once so popular, or if one surmises that some chess players gamble, internally, on one or another of a number of options, there still resounds a fairly justified chorus of affirmation that the two activities are opposed.

Duchamp not only liked gambling, but indulged in the last, best hope of the true gambler (which he does not seem to have been) and tried to invent the perfect system. He wrote to friends from Monte Carlo: "I have studied the system a good deal, basing myself on my bad experiences of last year. Don't be skeptical, since this time I believe I have eliminated the word Chance. I would like to force roulette to become a game of chess."

He even promoted a company, inviting investors to place their stakes with him, offering them 20 percent return on their money. In his prospectus, the Monte Carlo bill, he correctly added that "if anyone is in the business of buying art curiosities as an investment, here is his chance to invest in a perfect masterpiece. Marcel's signature alone is worth much more than the 50 francs asked for the share."[14]

But if he wanted to force roulette to become a game of chess, he also wanted the reverse. A contemporary reports that "when he was at Monte Carlo experimenting with his system he wrote to Jacques Duchamp, 'I would like to force roulette to become a game of chess.' When I told Duchamp that I did not fully grasp the relationship between chess and gambling, since the former involves the mind and the latter chance, he replied, 'In both cases it is a fight between two human beings, and by introducing more chance into chess and by reducing the chance factor in gambling, the two activities could meet somehow.' "

We are now in a position to review certain antinomies reflected in Duchamp's career and preoccupations:

ARTIST VERSUS BOURGEOIS. Duchamp was a dandy, a cultivated Bohemian. He attacked bourgeois ideas of art all his life, yet found that the bourgeois eagerly wanted to buy such tasteless assaults. Indeed he produced them with the knowledge that they would be bought. Modern art, nominally antibourgeois, was the object of bourgeois desires and was appropriated by the rich. Chess, on the other hand, while nominally bourgeois as a pastime, could not be appropriated by the bourgeois.

ARTIST VERSUS CHESS PLAYER. The artist is traditionally expected to be a blinkered visionary in his studio. Yet Duchamp knew this not to be the case, since it was a short order for the artist to be integrated into society. Chess players, on the other hand, "are completely cloudy, completely blinkered . . . madmen of a certain quality, the way an artist is supposed to be and isn't."

SENTIMENT VERSUS CALCULATION (or body v brains). Duchamp loathed lushness, the presence of recognizable flesh and blood in his artistic work. The separateness of the Bride and her Bachelors is given the imagery of the machine and the object. Yet intentional artistic work involved the representation of forms, voluntary images which linked him as a person to the art object, since the object was the result of his intention. Therefore Duchamp turned to

CALCULATION VERSUS CHANCE. He created pictures by dropping threads onto a surface and fixing them in the chance form in which they fell. He fired matches daubed with paint at the large glass and governed some of the images by the points where the matches struck the surface. By turning to chance he wished to dehumanize decision. André Breton wrote in 1924: "I have seen Duchamp do an extraordinary thing, toss a coin up in the air and say, 'Tails I leave for America tonight; Heads I stay in Paris.'[15] *No* indifference about it; it is certain that he infinitely preferred to go or to stay. But is not the personality of choice, the independence of which Duchamp, for example, by signing a manufactured object was one of the first to proclaim, the most tyrannical of all, and is it not fitting to put it to this test, provided that it is not to substitute for it a mysticism of chance?'' Precisely: Breton put his finger on the important point. Duchamp attacked the tyranny of personal choice, the governance of sentiment or desire, or "taste"; and he showed that one could do as well with the indifference of the roulette wheel or the tossed coin. Did he with his "perfect system" at Monte Carlo not show that he had succumbed to the mysticism of chance, if only in the reverse sense of saying, like a million gamblers before him, that he had mastered it? Actually, Duchamp escapes by a qualification. He would like roulette to become like chess. Now originally we had

CHESS VERSUS SENTIMENT. Chess, said Duchamp, "is mechanical reality." It had the truth of the machine objects which he put in his art works, or signed as art works. But the beauty is even purer than in art. "It's the *imagining* of the movement or the gesture that makes the beauty in this case. *It's completely in one's gray matter*." But chess cannot be a matter of indifference—if one wants to win, or find the perfect or the most beautiful move—because one must *decide* what to do next, and so:

CHESS VERSUS CHANCE. But even if Duchamp could see that chess was not a matter of chance, and was passionately addicted to the game, chance still remained for him an important aspect of his life, since it was a metaphor for indifference, his version of Rimbaud's *dérèglement de tous les sens* ("disordering of all the senses"). Therefore:

THE ARTIST VERSUS CHESS AND ROULETTE. If only "the two activities could meet somehow." But the coincidence Duchamp found between chess and roulette was that "in both cases it is a fight between two human beings." What a confession for Duchamp to make, because we then have

EMOTION AND AGRESSION VERSUS INDIFFERENCE, CHANCE AND THE MACHINE. Duchamp ceases to recognize the sublimation that art, chess and gambling afforded him. Irony gives way to passion, indifference to engagement. But he is left with this antinomy:

USELESSNESS VERSUS UTILITY. As his art objects become useful to the people who buy them, as objects of pleasure or of exchange value, and hence useful to himself since he can support himself by their sale, he turns to chess which is useless and cannot be appropriated. Chess becomes a criticism of art as an activity, since the former is a starker statement of indifference to the world. But Duchamp continues to deal in pictures, to produce the occasional object. Furthermore the sublimation of chess is by no means complete so far as physical desire is concerned, since Duchamp remains sexually extremely active. Nor has chess become the final activity of the indifferent ironist. The final confrontation is

CHESS VERSUS ART. "I was highly attracted to chess for forty or forty-five years, then little by little my enthusiasm lessened." In fact, for an unknown period before his death Duchamp had been at work on the Keyhole painting, a highly erotic work, which went to the Arensberg Collection in Philadelphia at his death.

Some of the Dadaists ended their lives with suicide, the only solution they could find to the juxtaposition of the absurdity of art and the absurdity of the world. Duchamp was an ironist, and ironists are sensible. Duchamp never made the final commitment to becoming "a madman of a certain quality." Recall Frank Brady's words: "The initiated [chess players] are promised the destiny of having to live a monk-like existence and know more rejection than any artist ever has, struggling to be known and accepted." Duchamp was known and accepted as an artist, therefore the knowledge that one day he accepted that he could never become the greatest chess player in the world was not as wounding for him as it could have been if he had not preserved his art objects for the museums that he pronounced to be mortuaries.

Duchamp made an experimental study of himself as "a personality disengaged from the normal contingencies of life." Yet I would propose that "the leave of absence from reality" prescribed by chess was too much for him, whatever the satisfactions the drama of the board may have offered. It was an aberration for the most aberrant of artists. Chess was a *process* of suicide that in the end he could not endure. But he was an artist, locked into a culture. What of the professional chess player, pure and simple? What other options are there? What have the consolations of culture got to offer him?

CHAPTER EIGHT

The Games of Our Lives

It would be pleasant to terminate this account with the enigmatic, oddly frivolous character of Duchamp. He was the true twentieth-century artist who "played" seriously without becoming solemn. But there are some conclusions that must be added, though flagging readers are entitled to leave the ship at this point.

Hitherto I have discussed individual chess players, such as Morphy, and explored their motivations and neuroses. By an examination of the social history of chess I have tried to show the pressures that a game like chess can impose on its adepts. I have examined the career of chess pressed into national service and finally tried to indicate its relationship to another "vanguard" activity such as artistic production. Chess does pose general cultural questions. Yet it is—however preeminent its advocates might claim it to be—only one of many types of game or play. It remains to set it in some sort of context, before arriving at any general conclusions. Games, after all, can be images of freedom, images of fear, enactments of pain, anxiety, love, the desire for transcendence, an enactment of suicide.[1] They sometimes inhabit a universe only abutting on that of necessity and labor; at other times they merely parody that necessity to make it tolerable.

"Play," remarked Jan Huizinga in his famous book *Homo Ludens*, "can be summed up as a free activity standing quite consciously outside ordinary life, as being 'not serious,' but at the same time absorbing the player utterly and intensely. It is an activity connected with no material interest and no profit can be gained by it. It proceeds within its own proper boundaries of time and space, according to fixed rules and in an orderly manner. It promotes the formation of social groupings which tend to surround themselves with secrecy and to stress their difference from the common world by disguise or other means."[2]

Now it is apparent that this definition can be compromised in a number of ways. What does "free activity" mean? Does it exclude the element of compulsion that is evident in play? For children have to play, in the same way that we all have to dream. Do we automatically exclude from the world of "play" an activity that involves material interest or profit? We might well do so, but it is one of the complexities of play in the twentieth century that it can become impossible to disentangle profit and material interest from it. We can, of course, make a straight divorce as Huizinga does, but that leaves us with little sense of history, of developing—if odious— ideas of what play can be. Again, the roots of play might be found in ritual, which may have stood outside "ordinary life" but may certainly have been "serious." Finally, does "play" involve the fixed rules and orderly manner to which Huizinga makes reference? Or is he blending *play* and *games* to produce this definition?

Play is an emblem of freedom but in fact often becomes a ritual of constraint. Children play. But they also *play games*; and there is a slight difference. Games imply rules—even if voluntarily accepted ones—codes of conduct, self-mastery. The pure notion of *play*, unqualified, seems to imply something childish.[3]

What can people really do with their time—and nobody else's time—when they do not have to work? What is the real opposite of work? J. H. Huizinga claimed that, contrary to most definitions of play, there need be no dividing line between work and play; that there is a play element in many normal working rituals. This tendency has been developed much further by such writers as Erving Goffman and Eric Berne,[4] who use the idea of play and of "the game" as a dictionary to interpret many features of interpersonal transaction and social behavior.

Such analyses perform the same function as modern notions of recreation. They subjugate the idea of free time, of the leave of absence from ordinary reality by inserting them into conventional social discourse or performance. Recreation can mean—and generally does mean—little more than the hours when the worker rests up and restores himself to do more work the following day. The adjustment of people in advanced capitalist countries to more "free time" does not necessarily involve a destruction or negation of the work ethic. Advanced capitalist societies have produced their own definitions of leisure, their own ideology of recreation, their own philosophy of the game.[5]

With the word "game" we are getting definitions more specific than those readily available for play, recreation or leisure. This is not to say that "game" is not, these days, a portmanteau concept. Games have to do with pleasure, economic calculation, even the logistics of massacre. They are played between people for fun, or against people to hurt them,[6] or with people to repair them mentally or physically: a lunatic might play with his doctor for one reason, the doctor with a lunatic for another; they might even play by different rules. Games can be studied from an enormous number of viewpoints. The anthropologist, the sociologist, the psychologist, the psychoanalyst, the biologist, the educationalist—takes his or her cut of the action.

There are many basic definitions. In their book *The Study of Games*,[7] Elliott Avedon and Brian Sutton-Smith come up with the following: "At its most elementary level then we can define a game as an exercise of voluntary control systems in which there is an opposition between forces, confined by a procedure and rules in order to produce a disequilibrial outcome." This suffers from the stuffed-suitcase syndrome, endemic to such attempts, but in fact the crucial words "voluntary," "opposition," "rules" and "disequilibrial" do produce a working model that is difficult to fault, though easy to build on. In the context of this study of chess with diversions in varying directions, here are some of the factors in game playing that interest me.

If games represent in some way an escape from working

reality, they are not an escape from *time*. Freud remarks in *Civilization and Its Discontents:*

> Order is a kind of repetition compulsion by which it is ordained once for all when, where and how a thing shall be done so that on every similar occasion doubt and hesitation shall be avoided. The benefits of order are incontestable: it enables us to use space and time to the best advantage, while waiving expenditures of mental energy. One would be justified in expecting that it would have ingrained itself from the start and without opposition into all human activities; and one may well wonder that this has not happened, and that, on the contrary, human beings manifest an inborn tendency to negligence, irregularity and untrustworthiness in their work, and have to be laboriously trained to imitate the example of their celestial models.[8]

One might imagine that in play and games we seek to experience time as an escape from the rhythms of the work place. But most games are tyrannized by time. Wherever it is practical, the stop watch dominates the proceedings as much as it does in an office or on the factory floor.

Next to the specter of time stands the specter of *utility*. People tend to shirk the question of utility in play and games. Beyond basic assumptions that games aid fitness or clear thinking one hears mostly banalities: games foster camaraderie, *esprit de corps*, togetherness, initiative, courage, decency, moral health and international brotherhood.[9]

One of the unpleasant features of this mania for conspicuous utility is the burden it places on the player; the public designation of what particular usefulness he is fulfilling may be entirely different from his own. Such contradictions can weigh disastrously on the player.

There is, though, in games a feature that is in contradiction to utility and the morality of time well spent; this is the role of *chance*. Chance, whether dictated by the dice, or by the weather, or by the unexpected frailty of a player is something that plays an equivocal role in games. On the one hand its presence, usually termed luck, provides agreeable dramatic tension. On the other, it seems to disturb the orderly deployment of skill. Thus, commentators often will remark that in such and such a game or contest "chance has been reduced to a minimum."

More fundamentally, chance brings us closer to magic, to prostration before providence. The dice or the roulette wheel are within certain perimeters, irrational; the gambler is not the pride of the sporting world even though he is an integral part of it. His vice, his lust to lose, his paranoia are more accessible than the inner torments or insanities of the chess player.

The best critique of Huizinga—and one of the most stimulating books on the subject—was that of Roger Caillois, in his excellent little book *Man, Play and Games*.[10]

Citing Huizinga, he remarked that "rules are inseparable from play as soon as the latter become institutionalized. They transform it into an instrument of fecund and decisive culture. But a basic freedom is essential to play in order to stimulate distraction and fantasy. This liberty is its indispensable motive power and is basic to the most complex and carefully organized systems of play.

Such a primary power of improvisation and play, which I call *paidia*, is allied to the taste for gratuitous difficulty which I propose to call *ludus*, in order to encompass the various games to which, without exaggeration, a civilizing quality can be attributed.[11] In fact, they reflect the intellectual and moral values of a culture, as well as contribute to their refinement and development." Now there is a certain optimism in Caillois's categorization of ludic play; a "civilizing quality" is attributed to it. Caillois protects himself somewhat by saying that unless it is social it is incomplete, a kind of makeshift device designed to allay boredom. One becomes resigned to it, while awaiting something preferable, such as the arrival of partners that makes possible the substitution of a contest for this solitary pleasure. In fact it is permeated with an atmosphere of competition, and unless it is turned into social competition it risks turning into an obsession for the isolated fanatic who would devote himself to it utterly and in his addiction withdraw increasingly from society.[12]

Merely by becoming social, ludic play does not lose the risks of obsession and fanatical isolation. Once again Caillois appears a little optimistic. In the case of chess, the social aspect of a two-handed game can merely compound the individual fanaticism and intensify it.

Beyond this point, how much activity does the notion of ludic play cover? Makeshift devices to allay boredom can include football, chess, drink, gambling, mountain climbing. Here Caillois produces four classifications of play:

The first is *agon* (Greek for "contest"). In a whole group of games that are competitive equality of chance is artificially created. The adversaries thus confront one another under ideal conditions. The winner's triumph, given the initial leveling of the odds and of the rules, is therefore estimable and beyond dispute. The point of the agonistic game is for each player to have his superiority in a given area recognized. The practice of *agon* presupposes sustained attention, training and, above all, the desire to win. The player endures discipline and is persevering. He obeys the rules. *Agon* can be expressed legitimately in competitive games such as sporting contests, billiards, boxing and, of course, chess.

The reverse of *agon* is *alea*—chance. *Alea* reveals and signifies the favor of destiny. The player (usually gambler) is passive. He waits for the cast of the dice. He risks his stake. Fair play, also sought but now taking place under ideal conditions, lies in being compensated in proportion to the risk involved. Every device intended to equalize the competitors' chances is here employed scrupulously to equate risk and profit.

In contrast to *agon*, *alea* negates work, patience, experience and qualifications. Professionalization, application and training are eliminated. In one instant winnings may be wiped out. *Alea* is total disgrace or absolute favor. It seems an insult to merit. It supposes on the player's part an attitude exactly opposite to that reflected in *agon*. In the latter his only reliance is on himself; in the former he counts on everything, even the vaguest sign, the slightest outside occurrence, which he immediately takes to be an omen or token—in short he depends on everything but himself.

Agon is a vindication of personal responsibility; *alea* is a negation of the will, a surrender to destiny. Some games, such as dominoes or backgammon, combine the two characteristics. And as I pointed out, chess until the fourteenth century was also split, some preferring the toss of the dice to intellectual decisions.

Agon and *alea* imply opposite attitudes. But they obey the same law—the creation for the players of conditions of pure equality denied them in real life.

Play, whether *agon* or *alea*, is thus an attempt to substitute *perfect situations* for the normal confusions of life. In games the role of merit or chance is clear and indisputable. All must play with exactly the same possibility of proving their superiority, or on another scale, the same chances of winning. In one way or another, one escapes the real world and creates another.

But there is a third way. The player can escape from himself and become someone else. This is a different category altogether—that of *mimicry*. In this play activity the player loses himself in the world of masks, and of disguises. He plays in charades: he becomes, in the old sense, a player in the theater. And mime can be expressed in another way—by the spectator of sports.

In *agon* the athletes do not perform the mime, but the audience, by sympathetically sharing in the travails and triumphs, partakes by an act of internal mimicry in their exertions. Of course, there is a reverse of this: that the audience does not participate, but coldly or neutrally observes—thumbs down.

The final category is what Caillois calls *ilinx*—in fact, "vertigo." This is not merely the miming of others, but the actual loss of self or alteration of consciousness. Children lose themselves by whirling around, until they fall. Later, at carnivals and fairgrounds people flirt with vertigo on roundabouts or Big Dippers. People who climb mountains or drive fast in cars all seek this sense of risky self-loss. People find it in the dance, in riding, in swinging, in watching people on tight ropes. Or they find self-loss in drink or drugs.

In these four categories of play activities there are two pairs.[13] In each of these pairs only one category, according to Caillois, is truly creative: *agon* in regulated rivalry and chance, mimicry in the conjuring of masks and vertigo. The others (*alea* and *ilinx*) are destructive. They exert a kind of fatal and frightening attraction, the import of which is to neutralize creative influence. In societies ruled by simulation and hypnosis the result occurs at the moment the sorcerer's mask becomes a theater mask: *ilinx* has become mime. In societies based on the combination of merit and chance there is a constant effort, and a corresponding transition, when justice is augmented at the expense of chance.

Caillois's final argument is that in the destiny of society, vertigo and the demons of possession are always being left behind. The group escapes from the kind of time that lacks a usable past or a sense of the future—a time in which it can only wait for the cyclical return of the masked gods, imitated at fixed intervals in complete unconsciousness of self. Men pass from the illusory, sudden, vain mastery of the universe to the slow but effective total control of natural resources.[14]

Now it is clear that Caillois saw a dynamic, historical development in all his categories: slowly irrational forces were—are—giving way to rational ones. There is indeed an implication that it is advanced Western society that is achieving this emancipation.

It is also clear that one can depict a greater element of "civilization" in all four categories. Thus, *agon* might originally have been a combat with rules and rituals—as described in Homer, for example—which would end in death. In *Beowulf* an aquatic contest is eventually resolved by one contender successfully holding the other under water until he drowned. Dueling, certainly a "game" at one level, was not a game at all for the punctured victim. Eventually only the sportive aspect remained. The original form of boxing perhaps terminated in the death of one participant. Certainly in the games of ancient Greece one pugilist was entitled to kill the other, unless the other succumbed. The exact level of control, or of civilization of the game, clearly depends on general social attitudes. The Romans were prepared to allow a gladiatorial combat to conclude with murder. In modern boxing there seems to me to be little doubt that the spectators, or some of them, would *like* to see the fight end in death, and occasionally it does. In that curious blend of *agon* and vertigo, motorcar racing, the spectator and the participant know perfectly well that the contest may end in death. Because bull-fighting is generally regarded as a "primitive" or "ancient" sport, most people dislike the evident fact that the bullfighter is courting death or conferring it. Disregarding humanitarian sympathies for the bull, who is the victim in almost all cases, we can say that motor racing is more sanctioned because the motorcar is at the center of our civilization and the bull is not.

The question really is: how long does a game remain "civilized"? Now Caillois implies that there is a general tendency toward civilization. Huizinga took a different point of view. The heart of his complaint, and indeed of a whole genre of complaint, can be found in this passage from *Homo Ludens:*

> With the increasing systematisation and regimentation of sport something of the pure play quality is inevitably lost. We see this very clearly in the official distinction between amateurs and professionals. It means that the play group marks out those for whom playing is no longer play . . . The spirit of the professional is no longer the true play spirit; it lacks in spontaneity and carelessness . . . The great competitions in archaic cultures had always formed part of the sacred festivals and were indispensable as health- and happiness-bringing activities. This ritual tie has now been completely severed; sport has become profane, "unholy" in every way and has no organic connection whatever in the structure of society, least of all when prescribed by the government. The ability of modern social techniques to stage mass demonstrations with the maximum of outward show in the field of athletics does not alter the fact that neither the Olympiads nor the organized sports of American universities nor the loudly trumpeted international contests have, in the smallest degree, raised sport to the level of a culture-creating activity. However important it may be for the players or the spectators, it remains sterile. The old play-factor has undergone almost complete atrophy.[15]

One can agree with some portions of Huizinga's argument, but dispute its basic premises, which are that there was a time when the pure-play element had not been corrupted, and that modern sport is not a "culture-creating activity." Huizinga detects play elements in curious areas—British parliamentary rituals of the eighteenth century, for example—and more generally he seems to be pining for the world revealed in seventeenth-century Dutch pictures, with jolly peasants disporting on the village green. With this kind of argument it depends what kind of play and what class of person you select. Jolly youths disport in Central Park every time I take a walk in it, but that pleasant phenomenon cannot be converted into a general historical judgment. Is he suggesting that "the great competitions in archaic cultures" had a strong "play element"? Unless one volatilizes the idea of play into an activity that can stretch from religious ceremony to chariot racing to parliamentary etiquette, it seems to me difficult to sustain a convincing argument, even though Huizinga's comments on professionalization may be correct.

Secondly it implies a limited idea of "culture" to say that modern sport is not a culture-creating activity. Sport manifestly *is* part of our culture, however reprehensible many aspects of it may be; and it creates values in our society however much we may dislike them. Huizinga, with his distaste for many aspects of the civilization he confronted just before the Second World War, seemed to wish to deny a phenomenon merely by averting his gaze from it.[16]

It seems to me more convincing to propose that play, in the variants suggested by Caillois, has always been present in history, either intertwined and confused, or sharply distinguished: that there is not "paradise lost" of play, or rather, that the "paradise lost" of play must be described in Freudian rather than historical terms. That is, "degenerate" or "advanced" play is not a phenomenon that has suddenly afflicted our civilization, nor is "virtuous" play something that we have suddenly abandoned; all the elements appear and disappear, arise and are suppressed, as historical circumstances change.

Thus, in the United States today one can find examples of all four of Caillois's categories; assessment of their banefulness or benignity must in the end depend on one's own political and social predilections. So far as *agon* is concerned, we have the vast public rituals of the national sports: baseball, football, tennis, boxing occasionally, basketball and the like. The development of mass communications (and of modern architecture, so far as stadia are concerned) has involved vast numbers of people as spectators. These spectators are part and parcel of the agonistic contest. The contest would scarcely exist without them, since they pay to view, and the players earn their pay by being viewed, either directly or on television. The spectators introduce the elements of mime, since they participate in the theater of the contest, at one remove. The contest is often aleatory, since people bet on the result, or in the case of horse racing, directly bet on the combination of agonal prowess achieved by breeding and training, and aleatory circumstance such as the vagaries of genetics, the skill or corruption of jockey and trainer. Finally, vertigo can seize the audience as it loses itself in the agonal contest and it can, as the commentators say, "go wild."

Alea—the appeal to chance—pervades society in the evident forms of gambling, lotteries,[17] cards, slot machines, the stock market and astrology. But it also occurs in what one might call the sophisticated appeal to chance, as exemplified in middle-class interest in the *I*

Ching or in the attitudes portrayed in Luke Rhinehart's popular novel *The Dice Man*,[18] where the hero satisfactorily resolves his doubts about the virtues of psychoanalysis by popping the whole problem back in the lap of providence. Decisions large and small are dictated for him by the roll and role of the dice. Nor is his technique a version of Freud's view that our *reaction* to a question asked of chance is what tells us what we really want. For Rhinehart's hero the whole of life becomes a game. Musing on life and modern man, he remarks, "To free him from his unending conflict we must urge him to let go, to act, to pretend, to lie. We must give him the means to develop these abilities. He must become a dice person." For the dice person, integrity means obeying the dice. "He feels *liberated* when he realizes his horrible problems are not *his* to worry about any longer; they've been shifted to the square shoulders of the dice. He becomes ecstatic. He experiences the transfer of control from an illusory self to the dice as a conversion or a salvation . . . the ego-control game is abandoned and the student surrenders to a force which is experienced as being outside himself."

For people in desperate need, chance may offer the only prospect of good fortune. For people without material deprivation, chance may salve a bad conscience and give the illusion of authentic living, since the "ego-control" game is abandoned. Of course, the ego-control game is not abandoned, since recourse to chance is an option, taken for certain reasons.

With mime, we start with the relatively uncomplicated world of the theater and the voluntary assumption of different appearances. Yet, without entering the world of role assumption, it is evident that much advertising is based on the supposition that people will elect to mime the images of satisfaction and plenty depicted on the television screen, billboards and the like. Sophisticated advertising even emphasizes this mime pattern, and playfully implicates the target in the theater of consumption that is constantly open to view.

Finally, with vertigo, we may start with the innocence of children whirling and progress to the alterations of consciousness caused by drink or drugs. The play, or leisure, of what came to be called the counterculture in the 1960s was closely imbricated with this desire to alter or elevate consciousness. So, whereas in the Soviet Union in the 1920s it was indubitably a progressive development to substitute the agonal activity of chess for the stupefaction of vodka drinking, it came to be thought in the United States that vertiginous play with drugs was superior to the agonal forms of play sanctioned by the state.

Obviously, in societies in a state of revolutionary turmoil, agonal play and games are regarded as infinitely preferable to appeals to chance, or recourse to self-stupefaction—ping-pong and revolutionary theater versus opium. Mime, to be sure, can take some strange turns, as when a vast mass of people (as in North Korea) depict, by holding colored pieces of cloth, the face of the beloved leader, or an imperialist airplane being shot down. But the option of *agon* as against *alea*, mime as against vertigo is not perpetual, nor static. One could certainly argue that the dope culture which expanded in the United States in the sixties was a progressive and necessary blow to conventional bourgeois standards, without endorsing the mysticism, quietism and solipsism that accompanied it, and without arguing that this need be the case forever.

Play and games are constantly in this state of flux and change, moving from a necessary activity to a sportive one—as in the case of bear baiting, which started as the necessary activity of the hunt, developed into the sport of attacking a chained bear with trained dogs and, in a final decline in the late-nineteenth century in England, involved dwarfs fighting bulldogs, an ancient working-class pastime to be sure, but not one whose passing I feel Huizinga would have lamented—or of a religious ritual into a playful one, or of a playful activity that may have started as childish frolicking, developed into a game, then into a sport. But the sport never remains static—just as the steel racket or the graphite shaft may inflect tennis or golf at the most expert level, so increasing professional expertise may gradually change the game into something unrecognizable to earlier devotees.

Now, although it has been emphasized that play is an absence from reality, this is true only on a certain level; absence from workaday reality might be a more exact term. Indeed, a basic point of this book has been that play and games are certainly not leaves of absence from the sociohistorical and psychohistorical environments that they inhabit.

Obviously, all games are suffused with a psychoneurotic content—this is as true of all games as it is of chess, though often not to the same dramatic degree nor with the same overt symbolism and evident results. With equal truth, play and games owe their popularity or decline to prevailing social and economic arrangements.

Thus much lamentation about the "decline" of sports into professionalism has really to do with lamentation that the development of a mass audience has made it possible for people to become proficient in activities that were once available only for those privileged enough to afford it—in terms of time or money or both.[19]

Again, many games are as meaningless as chess. Why struggle to hit a ball with as few strokes as possible round a carefully prepared course; or run five hours a day wearing weights in order to clip some seconds off a record; or hit a ball over a net for hours on end? Evidently for nominal pleasure, which could include social ambition, anal-sadistic satisfaction, the avoidance of boredom or despair. Some sports have more of an excuse— are at an earlier stage of development—than others. At one level the karate and kung-fu crazes reflect a feeling of personal insecurity; on another, aggressive fantasies. The former excuses the latter.

But at the most profound level—beyond the desire for "fun" or for exercise or for excitement—I think one can argue that games, with their own laws and their own time frames, represent an expectancy on the part of the contenders and of the audience; that games direct a question at the very heart of society and of culture as to what it could be and what it could become in terms of freedom and realized human potential. Some games are discarded, since the question no longer applies in the terms in which the activity posed it—as in medieval tournaments that asked which person was most courtly, which had the strongest horse, which had the toughest lance and the keenest eye; such a sport becomes an elegy for a class that has already had its day. Team games propose the vision of cooperative effort, and sometimes lose it in regimentation. The refinements of modern leisure marketing can preserve such games for a season if not forever.[20]

Now, chess is a paradigm of many of these themes. It is an agonistic contest, pitting person against person under conditions of almost total equality (excluding the fact that Black is at a marginal disadvantage theoretically to White). In its origins it contained the element of *alea*, or chance; it is a mime of the family romance and of the Oedipal drama; the concentration and dedication it demands pretend almost to the state of vertigo. In its early period it could be seen as a mime of the orders of society, but also an enlightened disruption of that order, since a pawn could take a Bishop, reason could triumph over rank. Yet, as it developed and became professionalized, it became "work," in which human creativity could enjoy ever-lessening triumphs—for, although the number of possible moves is virtually infinite, they are not absolutely so; theoretically there is the possibility of perfection, while actually there is the ever-narrowing practicability of arriving at it.

In the absence of joyful creativity, as memory and psychological endurance become more and more important, one might look for a mitigating social factor, such as public esteem and approval for the expert players. Yet—with occasional exceptions—they "know more rejection than any artist ever has." The world of the expert player becomes an increasingly hermetic one, in which the repressed matter sublimated by the game may return with increasing vigor and malignancy.

Thus, in the eternal unresolvable struggle of the two

sides we may see, not an image of discovery or a portent of the new, but what Luzhin, the victim in Nabokov's novel, saw to be "the full horror, the abysmal depths of chess"; a process of suicide; a mime of despair.

Notes

CHAPTER ONE. THE STORY OF A MERE CHESS PLAYER

1. From Frances Parkinson Keyes's novel *The Chess Players*, New York, 1960. This fictional account of Paul Morphy's life is full of interesting historical research and diverting incident. See my commentary on certain passages at the end of this chapter.

2. "He will plant the banner of Castile on the walls of Madrid amid shouts of the capture of the town, and the little king will take himself off abashed." In view of later commentary, a fantasy involving the King piece in chess.

3. Edward Lasker, *The Adventures of Chess*, New York, 1959. This is a delightful book by an enthusiast. He is no relation to Emanuel Lasker, the world chess champion from 1894 to 1921.

4. "There is no gap in the forest, there is no fresh trodden waste in the prairie which has not heard the name of the New Orleans boy, who left the nursery of his youth, like one of those fabulous heroes of whom our childhood loved to read, and came back, bearing with him the spoils of giants whom he had slain, after overthrowing their castles and appropriating the allegiance of their queens. . . . I propose the health of Paul Morphy, the world's chess champion. His peaceful battles have helped to achieve a new revolution; his youthful triumphs have added a new clause to the declaration of American Independence." Excerpt from the speech of Oliver Wendell Holmes at the dinner given in Paul Morphy's honor at the Revere House in Boston, May 31, 1859.

5. In view of interpretations of Morphy's experiences in Europe, it is interesting to compare what Morphy said about chess before and after his trip to Europe. In 1857, he remarked in a speech at a dinner of the New York Chess Club, "Chess, hitherto viewed by our countrymen in the light of a mere amusement, assumes at least its appropriate place among the sciences which adorn and exalt the intellect." In 1859, on his return from Paris, "Chess never has been and never can be aught but a recreation. It should not be indulged in to the detriment of other and more serious avocations—should not absorb or engross the thoughts of those who worship at its shrine . . . As a mere game, a relaxation from the severe pursuits of life, it is deserving of high commendation." The quotation from Staunton reinforces the argument that the latter had been Morphy's main target in Europe, not Anderssen.

6. See Chapter 7, Part 1, for Fischer's attitude to clothes.

7. Ernest Jones, "The Problem of Paul Morphy: A Contribution to the Psychology of Chess," *Essays in Applied Psychoanalysis*, Vol. 1, London, 1951. Even before Jones's paper, the Russian A. Herbstman had written on psychoanalysis and chess in *Psychoanalysis of Chess* (Moscow, 1925). Herbstman did not pick a particularly favorable time or place for his study, psychologically, given the somewhat orthodox Russian approach to chess at the time.

8. The expansion in the powers of the Queen piece came in about 1500, probably in Italy. Indian, Persian and Muslim chess had no Queen piece. Certainly the powerful function of the piece was created in western Europe. See Chapter 5.

9. Al Horowitz, *The World Chess Championship*, New York, 1973.

CHAPTER TWO. PATHS OF EXILE: NABOKOV'S GRAND MASTER

1. Robert Waelder, "The Psychoanalytic Theory of Play."

2. Vladimir Nabokov, *The Defense*, translated by Michael Scammel in collaboration with the author, New York, 1964. In his foreword Nabokov says that the Russian title of the novel was *Zashchita Luzhina* which means "the Luzhin defense." "The name rhymes with 'illusion' if pronounced thickly enough to deepen the 'u' into 'oo.' " Nabokov wrote it in 1929, and it was

serialized in the *émigré* Russian quarterly *Sovremennye Zapiski* under the pen name "V. Sirin," and was published as a book by the *émigré* publishing house Slovo, Berlin, 1930.

CHAPTER THREE. SPLENDORS AND MISERIES OF THE GREAT CHESS CHAMPIONS

1. Originally printed as Volume 3 of *Psychoanalysis,* the Journal of Psychoanalytic Psychology, 1956. Reprinted as *The Psychology of the Chess Player,* New York, 1967.

2. B. F. Skinner allows the children in his hypothetical commune outlined in *Walden Two* (New York, 1948), to play chess. It formed part of the behavioral engineering proposed by the commune's fictional creator, Frazier, "Every bit of our research, from the nursery through the psychological management of our adult membership, is directed towards that end, to exploit every alternative to forcible control. By skillful planning, by a wise choice of techniques, we *increase* the feeling of freedom . . . when we've once acquired a behavioral technology, we can't leave the control of behavior to the unskilled."

3. See, for example, the article in *Ms* magazine, New York, 1972.

4. In the *Adventure of Chess.* I have not dwelt in this book on the development of different styles of playing, on the grounds that this would be superficial for the knowledgeable and confusing for the tyro. Clearly there is an interesting area of study here—for example, in the development of the "hypermodernist" school, called by one commentator the "Cubists" of chess. There is a level at which style of play can be revealing about the player. For example, Lasker would complicate a position that might have seemed dangerous or hopeless, with the design that under time pressure his opponent would make a blunder. This tells one something about Lasker and something about the psychological strategies that are involved in the game. On the other hand, I don't think one can make too much, in terms of actual playing styles, of a remark like Spassky's about his incompatibility with his first wife, that they were like two bishops on the board destined never to meet. See the remarks about Fischer's Game of the Century in Chapter 7, Part I. Also Ben Karpman's review of Richard Reti's *Masters of the Chessboard* (New York, 1932).

5. *Conversations with Brecht*, London, 1973. Walter Benjamin writes, *"12 July*. Yesterday after playing chess Brecht said: 'You know, when Korsch comes, we really ought to work out a new game with him. A game in which the moves do not always stay the same; where the function of every piece changes after it has stood in the same square for a while: it should either become stronger or weaker. This way the game doesn't develop, it stays the same for too long.' "

6. My mother reports an innocent encounter with him. She was crossing the Atlantic on a liner in the early thirties. The stranger with whom she had a few moment's conversation in one of the saloons suggested a game, and she proposed chess. The stranger won effortlessly and then revealed that he was Capablanca. My mother then suggested the exciting game of balancing matches on the top of a bottle in alternation, until one or other player should blunder and cause the whole pile to collapse. She won three bouts of this in quick succession. Capablanca was in transports of excitement and suggested another round. My mother became seasick, but apparently Capablanca went about the first-class saloon for a couple of days asking every young woman he encountered to play the match game with him.

7. The exact villainy or otherwise of Alekhine is still a matter for keen debate. Soviet commentators are untrustworthy on the subject, since their account of Alekhine's actions has always been modified on the prevailing policy toward him as a national hero, as well as an expatriate traitor. See Chapter 6, on Soviet Chess.

CHAPTER FOUR. DEATH: ZWEIG'S LAST GAME

1. Norman Brown, *Life against Death:* The Psychoanalytic Meaning of History. New York, 1970.

2. This is quoted in *Stefan Zweig*, by Elizabeth Allday, Chicago, 1972. I have relied on this book for biographical details about Zweig. Many of Zweig's books are very much worth reading. His study of Joseph Fouché and his life of Balzac, as well as some of the famous short stories that interested Freud so much, are excellent.

3. *The Royal Game*, London, 1944. *Le Monde* serialized it during the Fischer-Spassky match in Iceland in 1972. The story is

accessible in Jerome Salzmann's handy compilation *The Chess Reader*, New York, 1949. This anthology also contains Ernest Jones's *The Problem of Paul Morphy*, as well as much other matter.

4. The quotations that follow are all taken from Norman Brown's discussion of the Death Instinct, in Chapter 8 of *Life against Death*. I have either quoted from or paraphrased many of Brown's conclusions and arguments. I would therefore direct the reader to this book, where Brown's ideas about the death instinct can be read in the proper setting.

CHAPTER FIVE. DOWNWARD MOBILITY: THE SOCIAL HISTORY OF A GAME

1. See for example the work of A. Binet, *Psychologie des grands calculateurs et des joueurs des échecs*, Paris, 1894. Or A. A. Cleveland, *Psychology*, Vol. 18, pp. 269–308. Obviously chess is of interest to those studying learning theory, or mental processes of calculation and recall. Writers of this type of study on chess have always been interested in powers of visualization, given the extraordinary feats achieved by blindfolded players. The world record here is held by Najdorf, who played forty-four games simultaneously, while blindfolded. The Russians ban blindfold chess, as potentially damaging to the player. Other areas of study have included memory and the alliance of chess to mathematical talent. But on the question of why a player like Capablanca should suddenly at the age of four be able to defeat his father, having merely observed the game, has never been satisfactorily answered. Clearly there is a type of innate talent for chess which can be developed or intensified depending on the psychic makeup of the child.

2. See, for example, *Scientific American*, June 1973. Computer designers are interested, in the cause of making better computers. Lay observers tend to see the computer–chess-player battle as symbolic of either the awesome powers of the human mind or the awesome powers of the machine. Since no machine can yet play advanced chess, the former view still predominates.

3. Norman Reider, "Chess, Oedipus and the Mater Dolorosa," *International Journal of Psychoanalysis*, Vol. 40 (1959), pp. 320–333. Also printed in Avedon and Sutton-Smith's *The Study of*

Games. This is one of the best studies of chess. It also has a useful bibliography. I have used it extensively in the first part of this chapter; I would recommend interested readers to refer to the original text for many of Reider's conclusions.

4. Loosely, "Family Romance" is often used to refer to the unconscious sexual tensions and conflicts arising from the desire of the son/daughter for the mother/father (and vice versa). Specifically, it is a term for the varied fantasies with which the child rejects his own parents by imagining that he is the offspring of other parents—exalted and noble. Among other functions, these fantasies lessen oedipal guilt by denying the incestuous quality of the child's libidinal feelings toward the real parents.

5. Most of the myths are recorded in H. J. R. Murray, *A History of Chess*, Oxford, 1913. This study is essential for anyone who wishes to study the history of the game, from the social, geographic, philological viewpoints. I have made extensive use of it in this chapter, as has almost every writer on chess.

The major source for thirteenth-century legends about the origins of the game (including the Evil Merodach story mentioned here) is Jacobus de Cessolis, *Liber de moribus hominum et officiis nobilium*. Cessolis was a Dominican monk from Lombardy. Murray says that his work was "the most ambitious and, from the literary point of view, the most important of all the chess moralities." It dated from the second half of the thirteenth century.

6. This view was advanced by A. Herbstman in his *Psychoanalysis of Chess*.

7. This story is included in the life of as-Suli the chess player in the K. wafayat al-ayan of b. Kallikan (d. 681), whence it was taken by as-Safadi (d. 764). The motive for the invention of chess by the Indians was the humiliation of the Persians, who had invented nard (Murray, p. 211).

8. Ref. Man f. 15a on the authority of b. Makhshari (Murray p. 210).

9. Told in Murray, p. 211.

10. Al-Mas'udi's account, Murray, p. 210.

11. See Murray, p. 210.

12. European chess is of Muslim parentage. The game was invented in India, probably in the seventh century A.D. Its westward diffusion was to Persia and thence into Muslim culture and thence into Christian Europe. The Muslim game remained un-

changed from 850 to 1575, unlike the rapid development of chess in western Europe; the medieval game lasted from about 1000 to 1500. The modern game then emerged, though the "old game" survived in many areas for a long time. The earliest mention of chessmen in western Europe is found in a will made by Ermengaud, a count of Barcelona, made in 1010—"I order you, my executors, to give . . . these my chessmen to the Convent of St. Giles, for the work of the church." Murray suggests that crystal chessmen bequeathed to the church were used for refurbishing such things as crystal inlaid chalices; the reason why so many church sets are incomplete. A second mention occurs in the will of the Countess Ermessind, in 1058—"To St. Giles of Nîmes her crystal chessmen for the board." Apart from these Spanish wills the next precise mention occurs in the letter of Petrus Damiani (1007–1072), Cardinal Bishop of Ostia, addressed to the Pope Elect Alexander II, and therefore dated between October 1, 1061 and 1062. This letter is quoted in the text below. Chess is mentioned in southern Germany by 1100, in England by 1140, in France by 1005, in Scotland by 1150 and in Holland, Scandinavia and Iceland by the beginning of the thirteenth century. Versions of chess are known all over the Asian land mass. See, for example, the letter of George Bogle, a Scotsman sent by Warren Hastings to Tibet in 1775.

> Among the Tartars I have met with some masterly chess players . . . The game's exactly the same as with us. They have no idea of our unsociable method of playing. When a Tartar sits down to chess, he gets surrounded by three or four of his countrymen, who lay their heads together and consult with him about the propriety of every move. I had nothing for it but to engage an equal number of Tartars on my side and so combat them with their own weapons.

Chess reached Russia, scholars suggest, along the trade route from Baghdad to the mouth of the Volga. It rapidly became popular among the people, despite pressure from the Church to ban it. The Civil Code of Ivan IV (1551) referred to "pastimes of Hellenic devilry" in which chess, dice and tables are declared illegal. The law failed. Ivan the Terrible died playing chess. Turberville's *Account of Russia* printed by Hakluyt in 1589 has this charming couplet,

> The common game is chesse, almost the simplest will
> Both give a checke and eke a mate, by practise
>   comes their skill.

In Russia Western chess starts in about 1700, at the time of Peter the Great. Murray thinks the old and new games continued to coexist for a long time. Under pressure of the church the Tsarist police often frowned on the playing of chess in restaurants and cafés in certain parts of Russia. However, it was a consuming pastime of the gentry in the nineteenth century, a point which might buttress some of the arguments about the reason for popularity of chess among certain classes at certain times put forward in this chapter.

13. See the abundance of scholarly research on medieval usage of symbolism. For example, Curtius and Huizinga: there were four ways of interpreting texts—literal, allegorical, eschatological and anagogical.

14. There are many chess incidents involving Lancelot in the medieval romances—for example, Lancelot arrives at Arthur's court and goes into the Queen's chamber. A page brings a chess set and puts it between Guinevere and Lancelot. She tells Lancelot to kneel and set up the pieces so that the situation will not look too suspicious to the ladies in waiting. She unfastens her veil so as to free her lips for kissing. When the ladies in waiting are not looking, she leans over the board and kisses Lancelot. He responds passionately and scatters the chessmen. "Soft footed pages ran up to them and start to pick up the pieces like birds pecking at millet seed. In their corner of the room the ladies in waiting tutted severely." The Polish author Berent's version, quoted in *A History of Chess* by Jerzy Gizycki, London, 1972.

15. One could even argue that Morphy's preeminence came at a time when the Southern oligarchy was being undercut by the rise of capitalism in the Northern states, and by the draining of political power to the North.

16. "On the other hand the fact that a menial knew anything of chess aroused suspicions as to his identity. Huon of Bordeaux, disguised as the varlet to a traveling minstrel, found that his word was doubted when he boasted his skill in chess, and the Devil is discovered in the guise of a servant in Gautier de Coincy's *Miracles de la Sainte Vierge* (c. 1230) through his unusual accomplishments" (Murray, *History of Chess*, p. 439).

17. An exception seems to have been the French-Swedish film *Les Créatures*, directed by Agnes Varda. I have not seen this film, made in 1956, but the account in Gizycki's *History of Chess* makes it sound most interesting:

> The main character, Edgar, who is a writer, carries out an observation of the inhabitants of a small island near the coast of Brittany in order to collect material to work out the fates of dramatis personae in his novel. He becomes engaged in an extraordinary game played with the keeper of a lighthouse, inventor of a peculiar playing machine combining elements of chess, cards and dice, and provided with a radar-and-television screen projecting images from real life which resemble the situations of the chessboard. Animated tiny figures of people appear in place of chessmen. Cards decide which is to be moved on the board, and dice—by how many squares. In the display appear appropriate episodes from the lives of the small creatures, depending on which of the players influences the course of events. A further complication is that the creatures endeavour to escape the influence of the players and make their own "moves." At this game of "living chess" the man from the lighthouse represents "an evil fate." The game is played on his terms. To win the game, the writer has to save from destruction on the chessboard (and at the same time in actual life) at least a single couple—a man and a woman. The stake is the writer's wife. The finale: the writer who has had enough of playing with human life . . . destroys the machine.

Apart from the sentimental ending, this seems to be an interesting plot. "Living Chess" has always fascinated people—the notion of absolute power in the disposition of men and women; also the notion that a *wrong* move can cause death; in fact, eruption of the repressed urges to be found among chess players and games players generally. "In Spain, a Dominican member of the Inquisition, Pedro Aabues, ordered unfortunate victims of persecutions to stand in as figures in a game of living chess played by two blind monks. Each time they captured a piece, they condemned someone to death" (J. Gizycki, *op. cit.*, p. 197).

"The Royal Game" was made into a film with Curt Jurgens in West Germany. It does not seem to have been good. In 1925 V.

Pudovkin, with N. Shpikovsky made *Chess Fever*. It was Pudovkin's first film, and made with haste to coincide with the great tournament taking place in Moscow that year. Apart from the Varda film, the only one that looks to be of great interest is "8 x 8" made by the veteran Dadaist Hans Richter in 1957. Jean Cocteau plays a pawn who is promoted to a Queen. Otherwise chess is used in films to indicate thought, problems, villainy or Nemesis. See Roland Barthes' essay on "Romans in Films" in *Mythologies* (New York, 1972), for an idea of the semeiological avenues one could pursue in this regard.

18. This is Murray's paraphrase of the oldest of the chess moralities, *Quaedam moralitas de scaccario*, otherwise known as the Innocent Morality. This was extremely influential in medieval moral literature. See Murray, p. 530.

19. From the MS. which Maurice de Reval brought home from France. See Murray, p. 535.

20. K. Colby, "Gentlemen, The Queen!" in *Psychoanalytic Review*, Vol. 10, pp. 144–148.

21. This does not necessarily mean they had good characters or fine minds. Cumberland was one of the stupidest generals ever to have misled the British army, and Sandwich was the celebrated butt of Wilkes, the English radical. Sandwich said to Wilkes, "Sir, you will either die from the pox or on the gallows," thus allowing himself to be checkmated by Wilkes' retort, "That depends whether I embrace your mistress or your principles."

22. C. H. O'D. Alexander, *Fischer v Spassky, Reykjavik 1972*, London, 1972.

23. There is one example of the coincidence of chess and the death urge given in Stanislaw Strumph-Wojtiewicz's historical novel *The General of the Paris Commune*, quoted in Gizycki, *History of Chess*, p. 216.

> General Wrobleski, who survived the defeat [of the Commune] sought to forget his losses in chess. "He is surely courting death," said Robert in despair, when the General, deaf to all persuasion and requests, used to go off to the Café de la Régence to play chess with anyone who happened to be there. The Poles who used to come to the café watched him in dismay; this man who used to be one of the leaders of the Commune, and now seemed heedless of the raging terror.

24. One of the very few first-class films made about a game. The insights could not be bettered, with regard both to psychology and to milieu. See Ned Polsky, *Hustlers, Beats and Others,* London, 1971. Important reading for anyone interested in the sociology of games.

CHAPTER SIX. PROLETARIAN, SOCIALIST CHESS

1. My major source for this chapter, and the one from which almost all my quotations from Russian accounts come is D. J. Richards, *Soviet Chess*, Oxford, 1965.

2. The report was by I. N. D'yakov, N. V. Petrovsky and P. A. Rudik.

3. C. H. O'D. Alexander, *op. cit.*, p. 49.

4. Spassky's sister, according to Alexander, was a champion checkers player. No direct symbolism, but of some interest surely.

5. Quoted in Avedon and Sutton-Smith's *Study of Games.* The source they use is H. D. S. Heistand's paper "Foreign War Games" in *Selected Papers Translated from European Military Publications* (Washington, D.C., G.P.O., Publication No. XVIII, Document No. 57, 1898).

6. The original ranks in the seventh-century Indian armies were allegedly Elephants, Chariots, Horsemen and Foot Soldiers.

7. Scott A. Boorman, *The Protracted Game: A Wei-Chi Interpretation of Maoist Revolutionary Strategy,* London, 1969.

CHAPTER SEVEN. CHESS AND LIFE

1. Fischer made this reply to the question posed by James Burke in an interview on the BBC. Reprinted in *The Listener* (London), June 1972.

2. For the theory of the spectacle in bourgeois life, see Henri Lefebvre, *Critique de la vie quotidienne*, Paris, 1966. Also the writings of the Situationists.

3. It would be interesting to compile a list and analysis of such events and pseudo events in this century: the Dreyfus case (the first words of shipwreck survivors who had been adrift on a raft for many weeks were "What's happened in the Dreyfus case?");

the Lindbergh kidnaping; the Montesi case in Italy; the Profumo affair; the Ali-Liston fight; et cetera.

4. The sources on the Iceland event were innumerable, Francis Wyndham's report, included in C. H. O'D. Alexander, *op. cit.*, is informative and funny.

5. Quoted in Frances Parkinson Keyes's *The Chess Players.*

6. Ed Barrach in *Life* magazine, in an article entitled "Bobby Is Not a Nasty Kid":

> Fischer has a high and earnest respect for President Nixon. The other day *Life* photographer Harry Benson arrived from a White House assignment with a personal message from the President. Excited, Fischer listened with growing delight as Benson reported what Nixon had said, that he wanted Fischer to come and visit him, even if he loses, that he liked him, "because he is a fighter." When we left, Fischer's eyes were clear and the angle of his jaw was aggressive.

7. This is by far the best source on Fischer's attitudes up to that time. The interview was conducted in August 1961 and appeared in the January 1962 issue of *Harper's* (New York). It has been suggested that some of Fischer's distaste for publicity, or certain types of publicity, stems from the frankness of this interview.

8. Interview in *The Listener* (London).

9. The title "Grand Master" adds a touch of hocus-pocus to the chess scene, with its echoes of masonry, and the grandiose titles that small sects tend to confer on themselves.

10. Gabrielle Buffet-Picabia, *Some Memories of Pre-Dada: Picabia and Duchamp* (1949)—quoted in *The Dada Painters and Poets,* Robert Motherwell, ed. (New York, 1951).

11. Arturo Schwartz, *Marcel Duchamp,* New York, 1969.

12. *Ibid.*

13. Pierre Cabanne, *Dialogues with Marcel Duchamp,* New York, 1971.

14. To pay for a dentist's bill, Duchamp gave the man a check drawn and signed by him, for the amount required. Naturally the value of the check as a work of art was greater than the cash value indicated on it. Duchamp eventually had to pay a large sum to get it back.

15. André Breton, "Marcel Duchamp," first printed in *Littérature* (October 1922); translated by Ralph Manheim and quoted in *Dada Painters and Poets*.

CHAPTER EIGHT. THE GAMES OF OUR LIVES

1. The bridge column in *The New York Times*, August 4, 1973, was entitled "Suicide Play Is Often Rated Murder by the Opposition." *Aficionados* claim bridge as a supreme game, equal in status to chess for scientific enjoyment. Huizinga says of it,

> It is in this field [intellectual card games] that the shift towards seriousness and overseriousness is so striking. From the days of *ombre* and *quadrille* to whist and bridge, card games have undergone a process of increasing refinement, but only with bridge have the modern social techniques made themselves master of the game. The paraphernalia of handbooks and systems and professional training has made bridge a deadly earnest business . . . An enormous amount of mental energy is expended in this universal craze for bridge with no more tangible result than the exchange of relatively unimportant sums of money. . . . Proficiency at bridge is a sterile excellence, sharpening the mental faculties very one-sidedly without enriching the soul in any way, fixing and consuming a quantity of intellectual energy that might have been better applied. The most we can say, I think, is that it might have been applied worse. The status of bridge in modern society would indicate, to all appearances, an immense increase in the play element today. But appearances are deceptive. Really, to play a man must play like a child. Can we assert that this is so in a game like bridge? If not, the virtue has gone out of the game.

I don't endorse all this (see below), but it is quite right to emphasize bridge. It has a great many interesting features, starting with its dynamics as a four-handed, as opposed to a two-handed, game. Its consequent superiority to chess as a social game, with the same rigid etiquette, is evident. Sublimated adultery, et cetera, in the pairing system.

2. Jan Huizinga, *Homo Ludens: A Study of the Play Elements in Culture*, London, 1949. This is the best-known book on play and games—partly because it is elegantly written. But it is not the best book.

3. See Saint Augustine for some of the hypocrisies involved:

> . . . but we enjoyed playing games and were punished for them by men who played games themselves. However, grown-up games are known as "business" and even though boys' games are much the same, they are punished for them by their elders. No one pities either the boys or the men, though surely we deserve pity, for I cannot believe a good judge would approve of the beatings I received as a boy on the ground that my games delayed my progress in studying subjects which would enable me to play a less creditable game later in life . . .
>
> [*Confessions*, Book I: 10]

Quoted in the extremely interesting and useful collection of essays and comment *The Study of Games*, Elliott M. Avedon and Brian Sutton-Smith, eds. (New York, 1971).

4. See for example Goffman's essay "Where the Action Is." Interactional performance, so far as academic writing is concerned, is a mine field of hocus-pocus and metaphor dressed up as science. However, the reader may like to turn to E. Berne, *Games People Play* (New York, 1964), or to E. Goffman, *Encounters: Studies in the Sociology of Interaction* (Indianapolis, 1961).

5. Leisure has always been a relative concept. The early Church fathers often pondered what Adam and Eve did before the Fall. No one assumed they were idle. Saint Augustine said Adam devoted himself to gardening, "the agreeable occupation of agriculture."

6. It is interesting how often in films the idea of games as an exercise in sadism comes up. Recently in *The Last of Sheila*, written by Stephen Sondheim and Anthony Perkins (1973), by the agency of play and games the central character intends to pry secrets out of his victims. Sets are often strewn with Monopoly boards, Clue and the like, to set a tone of malign idleness. Villains, as I have said, often play chess. Heroes rarely do.

7. *The Study of Games*, see Note 3 above.

8. Sigmund Freud: *Civilization and Its Discontents*, London, 1946.

9. Utility:

> Although business games are only a decade old their growth has been rapid. One of the newer games developed at the University of Chicago perhaps portends the future. The game is called INTOP (International Operations Simulation). The increasing problems of international trade and overseas operations have stimulated the University to develop a game with a "rather high degree of realism . . . [that] brings out the fact that effective solution of business problems . . . requires diagnostic ability and conceptual thinking. . . ." Although there is little scientific evidence for the worth of these games, like the military games that have been played for centuries, their pursuit is apparently convincing to their advocates. Whether this conviction is based on a certain intoxication that goes with game playing or has the substance of their claims cannot yet be known. Though as a precaution, we should remember that for about a century athletic coaches have been discussing the character-training value of sports, with much enthusiasm and practically no evidence. Their enthusiasm has not abated, but the evidence is still practically nonexistent [*The Study of Games*, p. 307].

10. Roger Caillois, *Man, Play and Games*, New York, 1961. My debt to this elegant book is evident and attested in this chapter. For brevity, succinctness and stimulation it could hardly be bettered.

11. Caillois says that *ludus* is not the only conceivable metamorphosis or, in our sense, "disciplining" of *paidia*. Ancient China worked out a different destiny for it: the term *"wan."* Caillois says the word has the sense of nonchalant meditation, lazy contemplation, the casual caressing of a piece of jade.

> To begin with, [*wan*] includes child's play and all kinds of carefree and frivolous diversion, such as are suggested by the verbs to frolic, to romp, to trifle with, etc. It is used to describe casual, abnormal or strange sex practices. At the same time it is used for games demanding reflection and *forbidding haste*, such as chess, checkers,

puzzles and the game of nine rings. It also comprises the pleasures of appreciating the savor of good food or the bouquet of a wine, the taste for collecting works of art or even appreciating them, voluptuously handling or even fashioning delicate curios, comparable to the Occidental category of the hobby, collecting or puttering. Lastly, the transitory and relaxing sweetness of moonlight is suggested, the pleasure of a boatride on a limpid lake or the prolonged contemplation of a waterfall. The example of *wan* shows that the destinies of cultures can be read in their games.

In this case, the destiny of a leisured and privileged society.

12. Pure boredom has biological as well as cultural facets of interest. In *Scientific American* (January 1957), Woodburn Heron, in "The Pathology of Boredom," gives an account of an experiment conducted by McGill University psychologist D. O. Hebb and associates to obtain basic information on "how human beings would react in situations where nothing at all was happening. The purpose was not to cut individuals off from any sensory stimulation whatever, but to remove all patterned or perceptual stimulation, so far as we could arrange it. College students lay on a comfortable bed in a lighted cubicle for as long as they cared to stay, with time out only for meals (which they usually ate sitting on the edge of the bed) and going to the toilet. They wore translucent plastic visors which transmitted diffuse light but prevented pattern vision. Cotton gloves and cardboard cuffs extending beyond the finger tips restricted perception by touch. Their auditory perception was limited by a U-shaped foam-rubber pillow on which their heads lay and by a continuous hum of air-conditioning equipment which masked small sounds." The subjects could not think clearly about anything for any length of time; became rapidly susceptible to arguments for the existence of supernatural phenomena; became afraid they would see ghosts; tried counting into the thousands, re-running films in their heads; thought about the past; ran out of things to think of; became irritable; childishly easily amused; paranoiac.

The most striking result of the experiment is that the subjects began to hallucinate; see images; undergo the same experiences as those affected by mescalin—

Our subjects' hallucinations usually began with simple

forms. They might start to "see" dots of light, lines or simple geometrical patterns. Then the visions became more complex, with abstract patterns repeated like a design on wallpaper, or recognizable figures, such as rows of little yellow men with black caps on and their mouths open. Finally there were integrated scenes: e.g., a procession of squirrels with sacks over their shoulders marching "purposefully" across the visual field, prehistoric animals walking about in a jungle, processions of eyeglasses marching down a street.

At first the subjects liked these phenomena, looked forward to them. After a while they interfered with sleep; the subjects found they had little control over them. Subjects had aural hallucinations too, and felt there were other bodies in the cubicle, overlapping with theirs. Some reported feelings of otherness:

"something seemed to be sucking my mind out through my eyes." . . . When they came out for meals, they tended to be garrulous and attempted to draw the experimenters into conversation [reports Heron]. In moving about, as they were led to the toilet, they appeared dazed and confused, and had increasing difficulty in finding their way about the washroom.

Encephalograms showed that slow waves more usually present in sleep began to appear when the subjects were awake.

Heron's account is absorbing. There is, of course, a development of this kind of experiment: the interrogation and torture technique known as sensory deprivation; most recently used by the British in Northern Ireland. Hooded prisoners were leaned against a wall, which they touched only with their finger tips. White sound masked noise. By all accounts the victims found this intolerable and rapidly disorienting. The only connection with reality some managed to maintain was through assessing the blood-beat in their finger tips against the wall. This was a therapy. As a whole, the technique was extremely successful from the intelligence point of view. Many of the victims subsequently had nervous breakdowns. Heron's account is reprinted in *Mass Leisure*, E. Larrabee and R. Meyersohn, eds. (Illinois, 1958). A useful collection.

13. Here is Caillois's diagram of his types, in two matrices:

	Agon COMPETITION	*Alea* CHANCE	*Mimicry* SIMULATION	*Ilinx* VERTIGO
paidia tumult	racing wrestling	counting-out rhymes	games of illusion	whirling riding
agitation immoderate laughter	boxing billiards fencing chess	heads/tails betting roulette	tag, masks, arms disguises	waltzing traveling carnivals
kite flying solitaire patience crosswords *ludus*	contests sports	lotteries	theatre spectacle	skiing climbing tightrope

	CULTURAL FORMS AT MARGINS OF SOCIAL ORDER	INSTITUTIONAL FORMS INTEGRATED INTO SOCIAL LIFE	CORRUPTION
AGON (competition)	Sports	Economic competition Exams	Will to power Violence
ALEA (chance)	Lotteries Casinos Hippodromes	Stock broking	Astrology
MIMICRY (simulation)	Carnival Theatre Cinema	Uniforms	Alienation
ILINX (vertigo)	Speed/Skiing, etc.	Vertigo	Alcoholism/drugs

14. One interesting example of the move from the mystery of demonic possession to the rational act of mime is given by Caillois:

> In a police state the uniform replaces the mask of a vertiginous society. The uniform is almost the exact opposite of the mask, and always symbolises a type of authority founded on entirely opposing principles. The mask is aimed to dissimulate and terrify. It signified the eruption of a fearful, capricious, intermittent and inordinate power, which emerged to evoke pious terror in the profane masses and to punish them for their imprudence and their faults. The uniform is also a disguise, but it is official, permanent, regulated and above all leaves the face exposed. It makes the individual a representative and a servant of an impartial and immutable rule, rather than the delirious prey of contagious vehemence. Behind the mask, the face of the possessed, when repelled, can assume a haggard and tortured expression with impunity, while the official must be careful that his bare face reveal nothing but calm and rationality, the face of a person specially charged with administering the law. Perhaps there is no better or more striking indication of the contrast between these two types of society than in these two distinctive performances—one that disguises and one that proclaims—between these two on whom devolves the responsibility for preserving such contrasting types of social order.

One point: the two forms can cease to be distinct: C.R.S. police in France; masked soldiers in Northern Ireland; tac squads in the United States. Partly for technical reasons (tear gas), partly to terrify the opposition, police return at times to the masked form. The bland face of the unmasked policeman is most readily seen when there is general acceptance of civil function. When this is questioned, authority can retreat into irrationality and the mask.

15. Huizinga, *Homo Ludens.*

16. Some claim that Huizinga's most famous and influential work *The Waning of the Middle Ages* suffers from a certain romanticization of his subject—too much nostalgia.

17. Lotteries are the state's most sanctioned form of gambling,

a regressive tax on the poor. No doubt, modern communications will one day have all this wired up, so people can gamble through the TV screen. Then Las Vegas and roulette could really become the center of national consciousness and effort.

18. Luke Rhinehart, *The Dice Man*, New York. 1971.

19. Class war and social mobility through sport; perhaps, when the relations of production remain unchanged, one can divine developments in the relations of leisure. But productive relations remain central—with corresponding efforts to introduce harmless metamorphosis through "worker participation," "job enrichment," or even "workers' control."

20. Although games rise and fall, we can get a longer perspective from studying the oldest list of games in existence, dating back to the fifth century before Christ, in the *Pali Dialogues of the Buddha* (edited by Rhys Davids in *Sacred Books of the Buddhists*, London, 1899). The Buddha is enumerating the trifles which occupy the thoughts of the unconverted man. "Whereas some recluses and Brahmans, while living on food provided by the faithful, continue addicted to games and recreations, that is to say:

1. Games on boards with eight or ten rows or squares.
2. The same games played by imagining such boards in the air.
3. Keeping going over diagrams drawn on the ground, so that one steps only where one ought to go.
4. Either removing the pieces of men from a heap with one's nail, or putting them in a heap, in each case without shaking it. He who shakes the heap loses.
5. Throwing dice.
6. Hitting a short stick with a long one.
7. Dipping the hand with the finger stretched out in lac or dye or flour water and striking the wet hand on the ground, or on a wall, calling out "What shall it be?" and showing the form required—elephants, horses, etc.
8. Games with balls.
9. Blowing thin toy pipes made with leaves.
10. Plowing with toy plows.
11. Turning somersaults.
12. Playing with toy windmills made with palm leaves.
13. Playing with toy measures.

14/15. Playing with toy carts or toy bows.
16. Guessing at letters traced in the air or on a fellow's back.
17. Guessing a playfellow's thoughts.
18. Mimicking of deformities.

Gautama the recluse holds aloof from such games and recreations."

Index